BEGINNING PROGRAMMERS AND PROGRAMMING PATTERNS

BEGINNING PROGRAMMERS AND PROGRAMMING PATTERNS

BY

ELSEA ROSE
GRACE GREEN

KNOWLEDGE
BAKERS

KNOWLEDGE BAKERS

ISBN: 978-93-9001-395-1(HB)

Published by : **Knowledge Bakers**
Pune, India
Email: info@knowledgebakers.com

PREFACE

In the dynamic world of software development, mastering programming patterns is akin to unlocking a treasure trove of knowledge and efficiency. For beginning programmers, understanding these patterns not only serves as a gateway to writing cleaner, more maintainable code but also cultivates a deeper comprehension of the underlying principles of computer science. As we embark on this journey of exploration, it is essential to recognize the transformative power that programming patterns hold in shaping the way we approach problem-solving and software design.

This book, "Beginning Programmers and Programming Patterns," emerges as a guiding light for novice developers seeking to navigate the intricate landscape of programming. Through collaboration with experienced practitioners and educators in the field, we aim to demystify the concept of programming patterns and provide readers with a clear roadmap for their application in real-world scenarios.

As editors of this volume, we have curated a collection of chapters that introduce fundamental programming patterns in a structured and accessible manner. From foundational concepts such as loops and conditionals to more advanced patterns like MVC (Model-View-Controller) and Observer, each chapter offers practical examples, exercises, and insights to aid in comprehension and retention.

Furthermore, this book goes beyond mere theoretical exposition, offering guidance on how to apply programming patterns effectively in projects and assignments. Through hands-on tutorials, case studies, and best practices, we strive to empower beginning programmers to harness the full potential of programming patterns and elevate their coding proficiency.

As we embark on this educational journey together, we extend our gratitude to the contributors whose expertise and dedication have enriched this volume. We hope that "Beginning Programmers and Programming Patterns" serves as a valuable resource and inspires a new generation of developers to embrace the power of structured, pattern-based programming.

Elsea Rose

Grace Green

CONTENTS

PART III. PATTERNS REQUIRING KNOWLEDGE OF LOOPS, ARRAYS, AND I/O

PART IV. PATTERNS REQUIRING ADVANCED KNOWLEDGE OF ARRAYS AND ARRAYS OF ARRAYS

PART V. PATTERNS REQUIRING KNOWLEDGE OF STRING OBJECTS

PART VI. PATTERNS REQUIRING KNOWLEDGE OF REFERENCES

[PART I]

Patterns Requiring Knowledge of Types, Variables, and Arithmetic Operators

Part I contains programming patterns that require an understanding of data types, variables and identifiers, the declaration of variables and a basic understanding of memory, the assignment operator and its impact on memory, and arithmetic operators. Many of the patterns in this part of the book make extensive use of integer arithmetic.

Specifically, this part of the book contains the following programming patterns:

Updating. Solutions to the problem of how to update a variable.

Swapping. A solution to the problem of swapping the contents of two variables (of the same type).

Digit Manipulation. Solutions to the problems of extracting and deleting the digits of an integer (from both the right and left sides).

Arithmetic on the Circle. A solution to the problem of performing basic arithmetic operations on quantities that repeat themselves (e.g., days of the week, months of the year).

Truncation. Solutions to the problem of truncating an integer to a particular digit (i.e., power of 10).

The patterns in this part of the book arise so frequently that they are second nature to experienced programmers, which can be quite annoying for beginning programmers, who have to think about them every time they make use of them. In and of itself, this observation is evidence for the importance of studying both these patterns and those in the other parts of this book.

[1]

Updating

Every algorithm of any consequence makes extensive use of arithmetic operators, whether it is executed by hand or realized as a computer program and executed by a computer. However, the two are different in one very important way. Calculations that are performed by hand tend to progress down the page, using more and more memory (i.e., paper) as they proceed. Programs, on the other hand, tend to declare a small number of variables, assign values to them, and then assign updated values to them. This chapter considers different ways of updating variables.

Motivation

Suppose you are writing a program that keeps track of the age of your favorite relative. You might declare an `int` variable named `age` and assign your favorite relative's current age to that variable.

Now, suppose you need to perform a calculation involving that relative's age next year. Obviously, you know that their age will be one greater than it is now. But, should you create another variable for that value, or should you just update the value of `age`? In some situations you need to do the former, but, suppose what you need to do is update the existing variable. It turns out that there are a variety of different ways that you can proceed.

Review

One approach to updating that you may have already seen involves the increment and decrement operators, ++ and --, which increase/decrease their operands by one. So, for example, you have probably seen something like the following:

```
int     age;

// Initialize the age to 0 at birth
age = 0;

// Increase the age by 1 on the first birthday
age++;
```

What you may not know is that, in some ways, this is just one (particularly simple) way of solving a specific updating problem (i.e., in which the variable is increased or decreased by exactly 1).

Thinking About The Problem

The same result can be achieved in a slightly more complicated but, ultimately, more flexible way. To understand how, first remember that the assignment operator takes the result of evaluating the expression on its right and puts it in the memory location identified by the variable on its left. This is done three different times in the following example:

```
int     currentAge, increment, initialAge;

initialAge = 0;
increment = 1;
currentAge = initialAge + increment;
```

These three assignment statements are particularly easy to understand because the expression on the right side of the assignment operator does not involve the variable on the left side. However nothing about the syntax of assignment statements prevents this from being the case. For example, consider the following statement:

```
// Add age and 1 and assign the result to age
age = age + 1;
```

This statement first adds the value in the memory location

identified by `age` and the value `1` and then assigns the result to the memory location identified by `age`.[1] In other words, it does the same thing as `++age`.

To the non-programmer this statement looks like a mistake because the non-programmer thinks that it says "`age` equals `age` plus one", which clearly can't be true. However, that's not what it says at all. It actually says "add the value in the memory location identified by `age` and the value one, and put the result in the memory location identified by `age`".

The Pattern

This idea can be generalized in a variety of ways by recognizing that the important pattern is the presence of the left-side operand on the right side of the assignment operator. In a fairly abstract way, the pattern can be written (in pseudo-code) as follows:

```
value = value operator adjustment
```

where `value` denotes the variable being updated, `=` denotes the assignment operator, `operator` denotes a binary operator, and `adjustment` represents the "amount" of the adjustment. Since `operator` has higher precedence than `=`, it is evaluated first. Then, the result of that evaluation (which involves `value`) is assigned to `value`.

This pattern is so common, that experienced programmers neither think about it themselves nor think to mention it to beginning programmers, but it's not as obvious as everyone makes it out to be.

Examples

You will encounter many situations in which you must keep track of something that is changing, but, regardless of its value,

1. This sentence is worded very carefully, and it is important to understand why. Note that it does not say "it adds the value 1 **to** the value in the memory location identified by `age`". It is the assignment operator, not the addition operator, that changes the value in the memory location identified by `age`.

you want to use the same name/identifier. In the example above, you needed to keep track of a relative's age over time, but you only needed their current age. In another program you may need to keep track of someone's bank balance as it changes over time, but you only need the current balance. In still another program, you may need to keep track of the elevation of a highway as it changes over space, but you only need the elevation at one location.

A Gradebook Program

Suppose you have to write a program that manages the grades that a student receives in a course. After the initial grade is assigned, you must deduct the late penalty (which may, of course, be zero). You can implement this as follows:

```
// Assign the initial grade
grade = 85;

// Reduce a grade by a late penalty
grade = grade - latePenalty;
```

A Retail Sales Program

Now, suppose you have to write a program that offers frequent buyers a 25% discount when they check out. You could solve this problem as follows:

```
// Offer a 25% discount
price = price - 0.25*price;
```

Because the `*` operator has the highest precedence, it is evaluated first.[2] Then, the result of the multiplication operation is subtracted from the `price` (without changing the contents of any of the variables). Finally, the result of the subtraction operation is assigned to the variable named `price`.

Suppose that `price` initially contains the value `40.0`. Then, this statement can be visualized as in Figure 1.1.

2. Remember, you can also use parentheses to influence the order in which operators are evaluated. For example, in this case, one could avoid any confusion by writing `price = price - (0.25 * price);` This is a question of style and doesn't change the pattern.

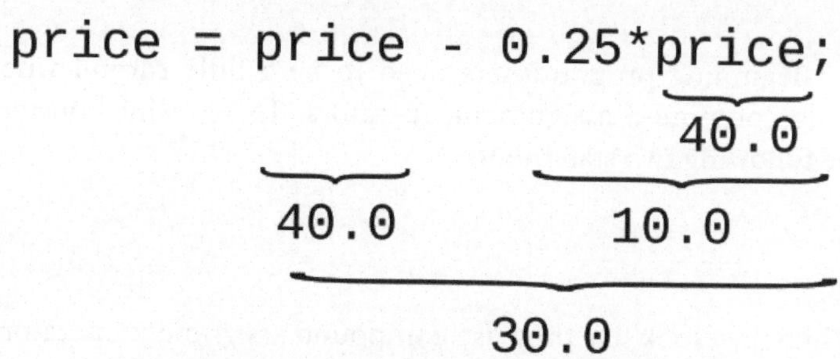

Figure 1.1. An Example of Updating

A Banking Program

As one more example, suppose you have to write a program that updates an account holder's bank balance. Assuming an interest rate of 5%, the new balance will equal the old balance plus 5% of the old balance You could solve this problem as you did for the retail sales program, but you could also do a little algebra "off line", observe that `balance + 0.05 * balance` is equivalent to `1.05 * balance`, and implement the solution as follows:

```
// Earn 5% interest
balance = 1.05 * balance;
```

A Warning

This pattern is so common that many programming languages include *compound assignment operators* to make it even easier to use. Such operators consist of multiple characters: the symbol for the arithmetic operator followed immediately by the symbol for the assignment operator. Note that, since a compound operator is an operator, it cannot contain white space (e.g., spaces, tabs, carriage returns, line feeds) between the characters. For example, the grading and banking examples can be written using compound assignment operators as follows:

```
// Reduce a grade by a late penalty
grade -= latePenalty;
```

```
// Earn 5% interest
balance *= 1.05;
```

Beginning programmers need to be a little careful when using compound assignment operators. To see why, consider the following two statements:

```
i =+ 1;

j =- 1;
```

While they look like they use compound assignment operators, they do not — compound assignment operators end with the character that is used for the assignment operator, they don't start with it. That is, += is a compound assignment operator, but =+ is not.

However, both of these statements are syntactically valid and, hence, will compile. This is because they use the assignment operator (i.e., =) followed be the unary "positive" (i.e., +) or "negative" (i.e., -) operators, without any white space between them. That is, they are the same as the following two statements:

```
i = +1;

j = -1;
```

just with different spacing.

[2]

Swapping

Programs commonly need to swap the contents of two variables. While this probably seems simple at first glance, it's actually a little more complicated than it seems.

Motivation

Suppose, for example, that you are writing a fantasy role playing game. In such games, players commonly acquire items of various kinds (e.g., weapons, spells, gold, food). When they acquire such an item, a representation of it (e.g., a `'T'` character for a teleportation spell) is assigned to a variable of appropriate type (e.g., a `char` variable named `spell`). As the game progresses, two players meet and realize that it would benefit both of them to swap their spells. This chapter considers a sequence of statements that can be used to solve this problem.

Review

There are a couple of things to recall in this regard. First, remember that the assignment operator (i.e., the `=` operator), stores the right side operand in the memory location identified by the left side operand. So, the statements in the following fragment:

```
char swordOfAlice, swordOfBetty;
```

```
swordOfAlice = 'C'; // Caladbolg
swordOfBetty = 'D'; // Durendal
```

can be visualized as in Figure 2.1. The first assignment statement stores the binary representation of the character `'C'` (i.e., `01000011` using an ASCII representation) into the memory location identified by `swordOfAlice` and the second assignment statement stores the binary representation of the character `'D'` (i.e., `01000100` using an ASCII representation) into the memory location identified by `swordOfAlice`.

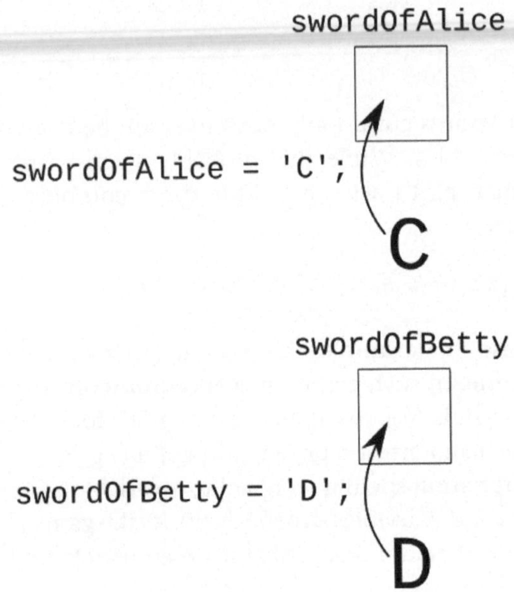

Figure 2.1. A Visualization of Two Assignment Statements

Second, remember that a variable can hold only one "thing" (either a value or a reference, depending on the type of the variable). So, the statements in the following fragment:

```
swordOfAlice = swordOfBetty;
swordOfBetty = swordOfAlice;
```

can be visualized as in Figure 2.2. The first assignment

statement stores the current contents[1] of `swordOfBetty` (i.e., a `'D'`) in the memory location identified by `swordOfAlice`. The second assignment statement stores the current contents of `swordOfAlice` (i.e., now a `'D'`) in the memory location identified by `swordOfBetty`. In other words, these statements didn't swap the contents of the two variables at all. Instead, the memory locations identified by both variables now contain a binary representation of the character `'D'`.

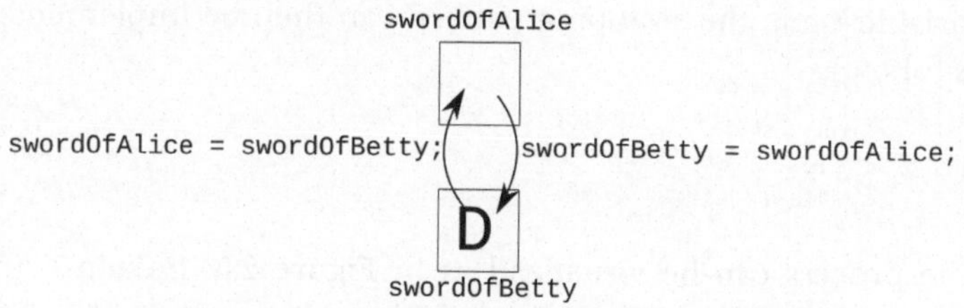

Figure 2.2. A Defective Swapping Algorithm

Thinking About The Problem

One way to think about solving the swapping problem is to imagine a situation in which you have Caladbolg in your left hand and Durendal in your right hand and you now want to swap the two. Since both of your hands are already full, there's no way for you to make any progress. To make progress, you need a place where you can temporarily store one of the swords. For example, you can place Caladbolg on a table, move Durendal from your right hand to your left hand, and then pick up Caladbolg with your right hand.

Note that this situation is not completely analogous to the way assignment works because the assignment operator replaces the current contents of the memory identified by a variable with a **copy** of the right side operand. However, it does

1. The use of the plural noun "contents" rather than "content" may be a little confusing to some readers. Though a variable holds a single thing, it is a kind of container, and we normally talk about the "contents" of a container.

provide the foundation of a pattern that can be used to solve the swapping problem.

The Pattern

Suppose you want to swap the contents of two memory locations identified by a and b (or, more succinctly, suppose you want to swap the contents of two variables, a and b). Before starting, you need a memory location that can be used to temporarily store the contents of either a or b. Calling that variable temp, the swapping pattern can then be implemented as follows:

```
temp = a;
a = b;
b = temp;
```

The process can be visualized as in Figure 2.3. In step 1, the contents of a is temporarily stored in the memory location identified by temp. In step 2, the contents of b is stored in the memory location identified by a. Finally, in step 3, the contents of temp is stored in the memory location identified by b.

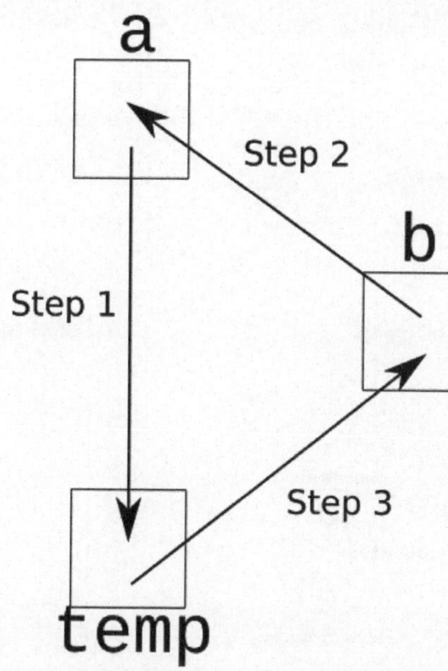

Figure 2.3. A Visualization of the Swapping Pattern

Examples

It's instructive to use the pattern to swap swords, carefully illustrating what happens step by step. The statements needed to conduct the swap are contained in the following fragment:

```
temp = swordOfAlice;
swordOfAlice = swordOfBetty;
swordOfBetty = temp;
```

Before the swap, the memory location identified by `swordOfAlice` contains the character `'C'`, the memory location identified by `swordOfBetty` contains the character `'D'`, and the memory location identified by `temp` doesn't contain anything (or contains "garbage", depending on your perspective). This is illustrated in Figure 2.4a.

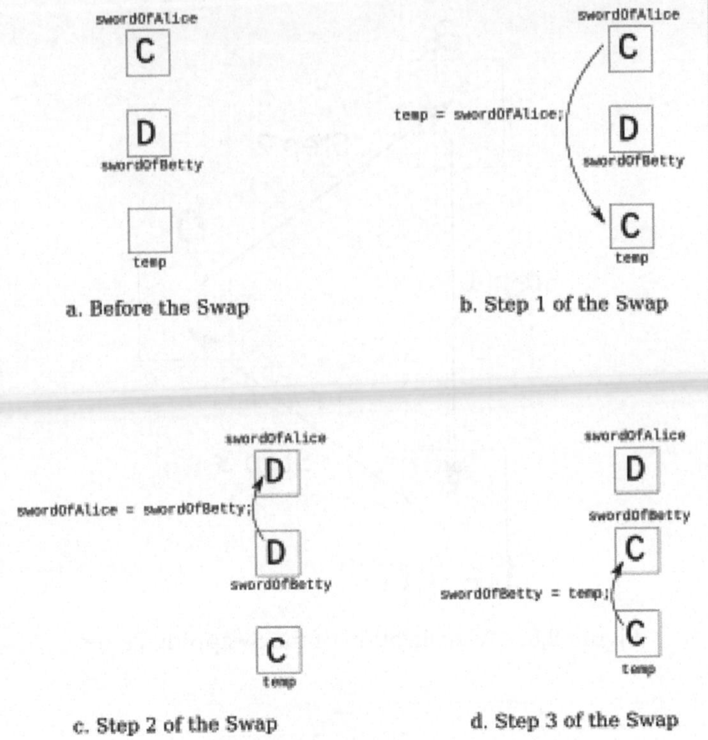

Figure 2.4. Steps in a Swap

In step 1, the contents of `swordOfAlice` is assigned to `temp`. Hence, both `temp` and `swordOfAlice` now contain a `'C'`. The assignment statement and its result are illustrated in Figure 2.4b. In step 2, the contents of `swordOfBetty` is assigned to `swordOfAlice`. Hence, both `swordOfAlice` and `swordOfBetty` now contain a `'D'`. The assignment statement and its result are illustrated in Figure 2.4c. In step 3, the contents of `temp` is assigned to `swordOfBetty`. Hence, both `swordOfBetty` and `temp` now contain a `'C'`. The assignment statement and its result are illustrated in Figure 2.4d. The result is that, as desired, `swordOfAlice` now contains a `'D'` and `swordOfBetty` now contains a `'C'`.

A Warning

At this point, if you know about methods, you might be tempted to write a `swap()` method so that you don't have to duplicate this code every time you want to swap the contents of two variables. However, though your motivations are to be applauded, it would be ill-advised to do so.

It turns out that there are different ways to pass parameters to methods, and the approach used in a particular language has a dramatic impact on the way in which one should implement a `swap()` method (and, indeed, whether it's even possible to do so). So, until you fully understand parameter passing, you may need to have duplicate code in your programs. That said, **be careful** — it's easy to make subtle mistakes when you cut and paste code fragments and then rename variables.

[3]

Digit Manipulation

In most programming languages, integer types (e.g., `int` in Java) are *atomic*. That is, they do not have constituent parts.[1] However, there are many situations in which one needs to manipulate the individual digits of an integer value. This chapter considers different ways of doing so.

Motivation

Suppose you are writing a program for a credit card company that has accounts of various kinds. All account numbers are nine digits long, they never start with a 0, the left-most three digits represent the issuing bank, and the right-most digit indicates the type of account (e.g., debit, credit, crypto currency).

Because account numbers are nine digits long, and the maximum `int` value is $2^{31} - 1$ (or $2,147,483,647$), you decide to represent each account number as an `int`. However, you realize that this means that you will need to extract digits from the account number, both from the left and from the right. In other words, you need to solve some digit manipulation problems.

1. Of course, we now know that an atom does have constituent parts. The term "atomic" is used for historical reasons.

Review

Recall that in a decimal (i.e., base 10) representation of a number, each digit is multiplied by a power of 10. The right-most digit is multiplied by 10^0 (i.e., 1, and hence is often called the "ones place"), the second digit from the right is multiplied by 10^1 (i.e., 10, and hence is often called the "tens place"), and, in general, the digit in position n (counting from the right, **starting at 0**)[2] This is illustrated in Figure 3.1. is multiplied by 10^n.

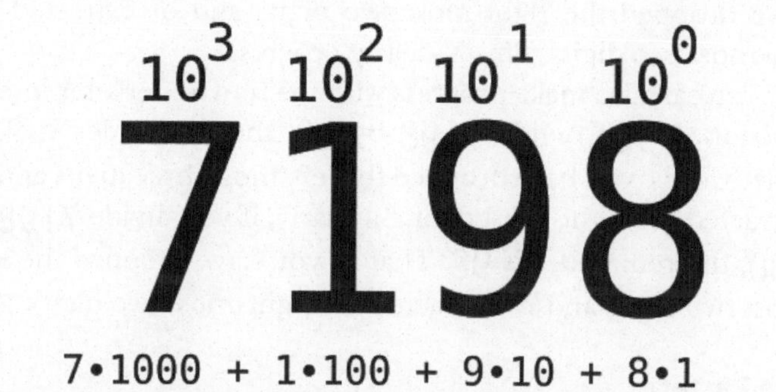

Figure 3.1. Decimal Representation of an Integer

Thinking About The Problem

Since each digit in a base 10 representation of an `int` corresponds to a power of 10, you should now be thinking, at least at an intuitive level, that solutions to digit manipulation problems will involve the powers of 10. The other thing that should be clear, again at an intuitive level, is that solutions to the digit manipulation problem will involve one or more of the arithmetic operations that can be performed on `int` values.

You can rule out addition and multiplication almost immediately, since both operations make the number larger. Subtraction might work, but it doesn't get you very far. Suppose,

2. You could, alternatively, start counting at 1 and multiply by 10^{n-1}.

for example, you wanted to get the right-most digit of 7198. You'd need to subtract 7190, which requires knowledge of the three left-most digits (multiplied by 10). Similarly, to get the left-most digit, you'd need to subtract 198, the three right-most digits, and then divide by 1000. The two operations left to consider are integer division and the remainder after integer division.

If you divide 7198 by 10 (using integer division) you are left with 719. In other words, you have dropped the right-most digit and/or extracted the left-most three digits. Similarly, if you divide 7198 by 100 you are left with 71. In other words, you have dropped the right-most two digits and/or extracted the left-most two digits. This is clearly progress.

You can also make progress with the remainder after integer division. If you divide 7198 by 10, the remainder is 8. In other words, you have dropped the left-most three digits and/or extracted the right-most digit. Similarly, if you divide 7198 by 100, the remainder is 98. That is, you have dropped the left-most two digits and/or extracted the right-most two digits.

The Pattern

One aspect of the pattern should now be relatively easy to see, the operation. To drop from the right or extract from the left you must use integer division. On the other hand, to extract from the right or drop from the left you must use the remainder after integer division.

The simpler cases involve counting from the right, and can be handled as follows:

- To drop the n right-most digits from a number you must divide by 10^n.
- To extract the n right-most digits from a number you must find the remainder after dividing by 10^n.

Extracting digits on the left and dropping digits on the left are both slightly more complicated because these operations require knowledge of the number of digits in the number as well as the number of digits to extract or drop. Letting N denote the number of digits in the number, the pattern can be completed as follows:

- To extract the n left-most digits from a number you must divide by 10^{N-n}.
- To drop the n left-most digits from a number you must find the remainder after dividing by 10^{N-n}.

Examples

Returning to the credit card example, suppose the account number is 412831758. To extract the card type from the account number you need to extract the right-most digit. This means that you must find the remainder after dividing by 10^1 (or 10). You can accomplish this as follows:

```
cardNumber  = 412831758;
accountType = cardNumber % 10; // Extract right-most 1 digit
```

To extract the issuing bank number you must extract the left-most three digits of a nine digit number. This means that you must divide by 10^{9-3}, or 10^6, or 1000000. This can be accomplished as follows:

```
cardNumber = 412831758;
issuer     = cardNumber / 1000000; // Extract left-most 3 (of 9) digits
```

The part of the account number that identifies the account holder consists of the remaining digits. To get this part of the account number you must first drop the left-most three digits (i.e., you must find the remainder after dividing by 10^{9-3}). Then, you must drop the right-most digit of the result (i.e., you must divide the result by 10^1). This can be accomplished as follows:

```
cardNumber = 412831758;
holder     = (cardNumber % 1000000) / 10;
```

A Warning

You need to be especially careful about the order in which

you perform operations when using this pattern in a repeated fashion because they change the number of digits, N. For example, when finding the account holder in the example above you had to first take the remainder after dividing by 1000000 and then divide by 10. Had you divided by 10 first, the intermediate value would have been 41283175 and the remainder after dividing by 1000000 would then have been 283175 instead of 83175.

Reversing the order of operations results in an incorrect solution because the intermediate value 41283175 only has 8 digits, not 9. So, to extract the right-most 3 digits you would have to take the remainder after dividing by 10^{8-3} or (100000).

Looking Ahead

If you take a course on systems programming, you will probably encounter the following topics related to digit manipulation: working in other bases and bit shifting. Both are discussed briefly below.

Generalizing the Pattern

For reasons that may not be apparent now, *hexadecimal* (i.e., base 16) frequently arises in computing. Fortunately, this same pattern can be used with other bases. All that is needed is to replace 10 with the desired base, b.

Bit Shifting

For reasons that hopefully are already apparent to you, binary (i.e., base 2) is also very important in computing. Many programming languages (including Java) include the >> and << operators to shift the binary representation of an integer value to the right or left a given number of places. These lower-level operators are more relevant in a systems programming course than an applications programming course, but will be touched upon briefly at the end of Chapter 18 on segmented/packed arrays.

[4]

Arithmetic on the Circle

When children are first taught to count, they are introduced to the concept of a *number line*. That approach then subconsciously influences the way people think about arithmetic throughout their lives. However, one can also perform arithmetic on a *number circle*, which turns out to be a good way to solve an enormous number of programming problems.

Motivation

Quite frequently, values can be increased without bound. For example, if you start with $3.00 and someone keeps giving you dollar bills, you will have more and more dollar bills (subject, of course, to tax laws and the like). However, in some cases, values don't keep increasing, they "repeat" (for lack of a better word). For example, if you start at three o'clock (i.e., 3:00) and keep increasing the hour of the day, you will (in fairly short order) get back to three o'clock (ignoring the AM/PM distinction, for the moment). To handle these kinds of situations you need to re-think addition and subtraction.

Review

A number line is usually represented as a line with arrow heads at both ends (indicating that it continues forever in both directions) and labeled tick marks (indicating the integers). A traditional number line increases to the right and decreases to the left. An example, focusing on the first twelve non-negative integers, is illustrated in Figure 4.1.

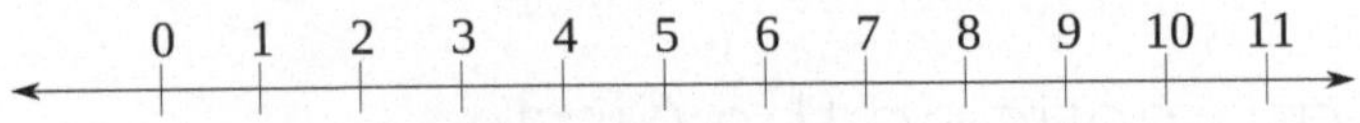

Figure 4.1. The Traditional Number Line

Addition on the number line involves moving to the right from a particular tick mark. So, for example, suppose you are interested in the quantity $x+2$. Then, you locate x on the number line and move 2 tick marks to the right. This is illustrated in Figure 4.2.

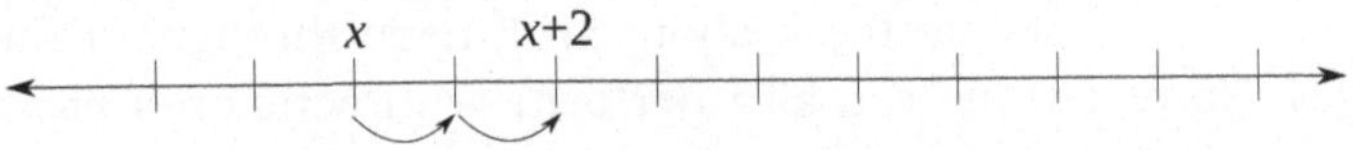

Figure 4.2. Addition on a Line

Similarly, subtraction on the number line involves moving to the left from a particular tick mark. So, for example, suppose you are interested in the quantity $x-1$. Then, you locate x on the number line and move 1 tick mark to the left. This is illustrated in Figure 4.3.

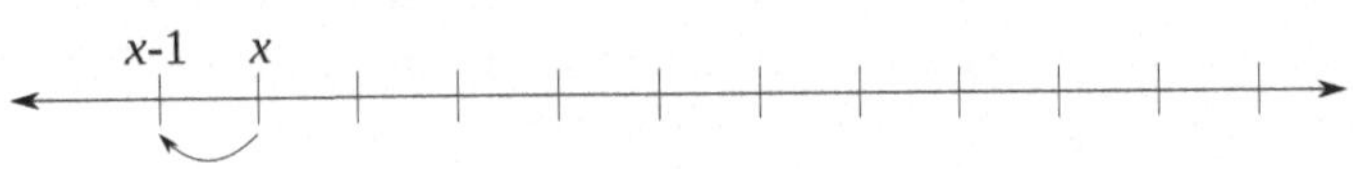

Figure 4.3. Subtraction on a Line

So, if you start with $3.00 and someone gives you fifteen more dollars, you will have $18.00. On the other hand, if you start with $3.00 and spend $5.00, you will have $-2.00 (i.e., you will be $2.00 in debt). Does this sound like elementary school? Good, it should.

Thinking About The Problem

Now, however, consider what happens if you start at three o'clock (i.e., 3:00) and add fifteen hours. You **don't** wind up at eighteen o'clock (i.e., 18:00) because there is no such hour (on a traditional twelve-hour clock). Instead, what happens conceptually is that the hour "circles around". Indeed, on a traditional analog clock, this is what happens physically, as well. It also provides a way of thinking about the problem — use a number circle instead of a number line.

A number circle is a circle with labeled tick marks (indicating the integers) rather than a line with tick marks. A traditional number circle increases in the clockwise direction and decreases in the counterclockwise direction. An example, which includes the first twelve non-negative integers, is illustrated in Figure 4.4.

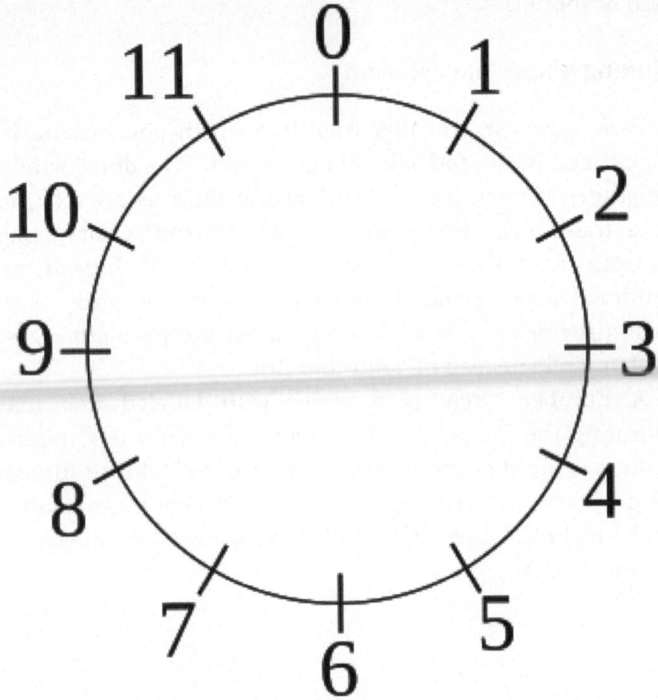

Figure 4.4. Numbers on a Circle

Addition on the number circle involves moving in the clockwise direction from a particular tick mark. So, for example, suppose you are interested in the quantity $x + 2$. Then, you locate x on the number circle and move 2 tick marks in the clockwise direction. This is illustrated in Figure 4.5a.

Similarly, subtraction on the number circle involves moving in the counterclockwise direction from a particular tick mark. So, for example, suppose you are interested in the quantity $x - 1$. Then, you locate x on the number circle and move 1 tick mark in the counterclockwise direction. This is illustrated in Figure 4.5b.

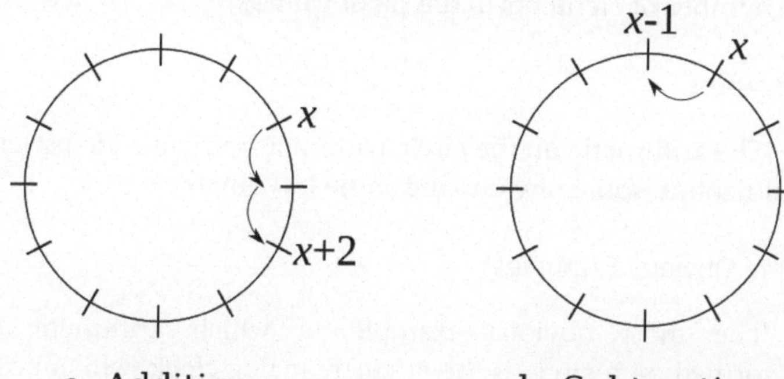

Figure 4.5. Addition and Subtraction on a Circle

The important difference between addition/subtraction on the number line and on the number circle should be readily apparent. On the number line the values are unbounded and never repeat, while on the number circle the values are bounded and (eventually) repeat.

The Pattern

The way to approach problems of this kind is to distinguish the number of times you move around the circle (which you typically aren't interested in) from where you are on the circle (which you are interested in). Specifically, the pattern works as follows:

1. Use a 0-based set of consecutive integer values.
2. Use integer arithmetic and the following variables:

```
int cardinality, change, current, passes, remainder;
```

3. If needed, calculate the number of times 0 is passed as follows:

```
passes = (current + change) / cardinality;
```

4. Calculate the `remainder` as follows:

```
remainder = (current + change) % cardinality;
```

where `current` denotes the current value, `change` denotes the change (either positive or negative), and `cardinality` denotes the number of elements in the set of values.

Examples

The arithmetic on the circle pattern arises in a wide variety of situations, some obvious and some less obvious.

Some Obvious Examples

The most obvious example in which arithmetic is performed on a circle is the circular, analog clock (which even looks like a number circle). Indeed, this is exactly the number circle in Figure 4.4, except that noon and midnight are represented as 0 instead of 12. To avoid both this potential source of confusion and the AM/PM issue, consider, instead, a clock that uses military time. In such a clock, midnight is "0 hundred hours", eleven in the morning is "11 hundred hours", five in the evening is "17 hundred hours", etc. Such a clock is illustrated in Figure 4.6.

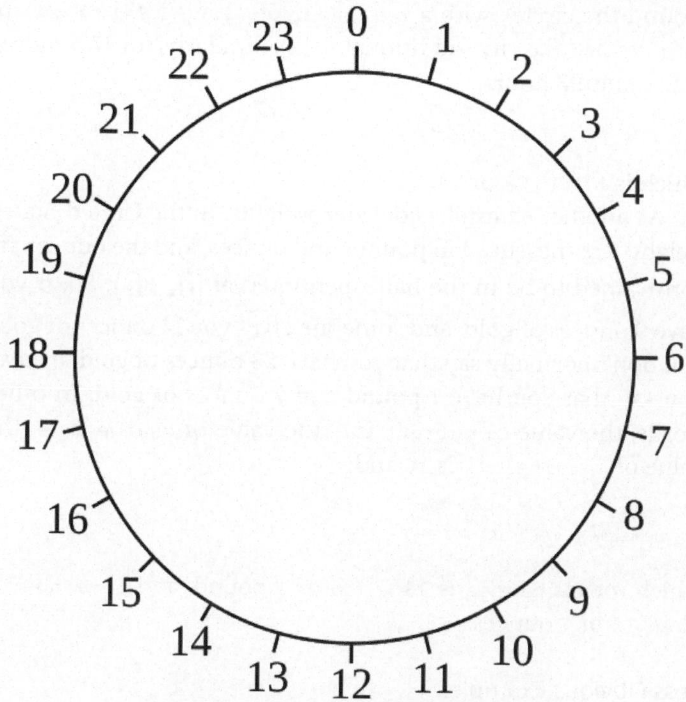

Figure 4.6. An Analog Military Clock

Some questions involving such a clock are easy to answer. For example, suppose it is currently 5 hundred hours, what time will it be in 8 hours? This doesn't require any thought; you can use traditional addition to determine that the answer is 13 hundred hours. However, some are more difficult. For example, suppose it is currently 17 hundred hours, what time will it be in 12 hours? Unfortunately, traditional addition is no longer enough to solve this problem. Obviously, the answer isn't 29 hundred hours, because there is no such time. Instead, you have to account for the fact that you've advanced a day. Even worse, suppose it is 17 hundred hours and you want to know the time 93 hours from now. Then, you have to account for the fact that you have advanced several days.

Using the arithmetic on the circle pattern, 17 hundred hours plus 12 hours can be thought of (using integer arithmetic) as a passes of ((17 + 12) / 24) or 29 / 24 or 1 (i.e., one time around the circle), with a remainder of ((17 + 24) % 24) or 29 % 24 or 5 (i.e., five additional ticks). Similarly, for 17 hundred hours plus 93 hours:

```
remainder = (17 + 93) % 24;
```

which is 110 % 24 or 14.

As another example, consider weights. In the United States, weights are measured in pounds and ounces, and the ounces are constrained to be in the half-open interval $[0, 16)$. So, if you have 9 ounces of gold, and someone gives you 14 ounces of gold, you don't normally say that you have 23 ounces of gold, instead you say that you have 1 pound and 7 ounces of gold. In other words, the value of current is 9, the value of change is 14, the value of cardinality is 16 and:

```
passes    = (9 + 14) / 16;
remainder = (9 + 14) % 16;
```

which means passes is 23 / 16 or 1 pound, and remainder is 23 % 16 or 7 ounces.

Less Obvious Examples

As shown above, arithmetic on the circle can be used with values that are naturally numeric, but they can also be used with categories. One common application is to determine the day of the week some number of days in the future. The set of days of the week (i.e., Sunday, Monday, Tuesday, Wednesday, Thursday, Friday, and Saturday) has a cardinality of 7. Using a 0-based numbering scheme, you can denote Sunday by 0, Monday by 1, etc. Then, if it is currently Wednesday (i.e., day of the week 3), you can determine the day of the week 6 days in the future as:

```
remainder = (3 + 6) % 7;
```

which is 9 % 7 or 2 (i.e., Tuesday). Similarly, the day of the week 516 days in the future is:

```
remainder = (3 + 516) % 7;
```

which is 519 % 7 or 1 (i.e., Monday). Obviously, the same thing can be done for months of the year. This set has a cardinality of

12 and a 0-based numbering scheme would assign 0 to January, 1 to February, etc.

Less obviously, perhaps, this pattern can be used for categories that are not normally numbered. For example, suppose you want to know whether a number is even or odd (a set with cardinality of two). Letting 0 denote the even numbers and 1 denote the odd numbers, you can determine whether the sum of two numbers, `current` and `change`, is even or odd using:

```
remainder = (current + change) % 2;
```

Further, since `change` can be zero, you can determine whether the number `current` is even or odd using:

```
remainder = current % 2;
```

which makes sense since a number is even if it is divisible by two with no remainder (sometimes called "evenly divisible by two").

This pattern can also be used for such things as determining which player's turn it is in a game, how to cycle through a fixed set of colors in a drawing program, etc. Indeed, this pattern arises so frequently that it is virtually indispensable.

[5]

Truncation

Integers commonly include more digits of accuracy than needed. In some situations, the right way to deal with this is using *truncation*. Truncation problems can be solved by dropping the right-most digits using the techniques from Chapter 3 on digit manipulation and then multiplying.

Motivation

Suppose you have to write a payroll program for a manufacturing company. The employees at the company get paid a fixed amount per piece, but only for multiples of ten pieces. For inventory purposes, the company keeps track of the exact number of pieces completed, but for payroll purposes, that number has more digits of accuracy than is needed. For example, if the employee completes 520 pieces, 521 pieces, or 529 pieces, they are going to be payed for 520 pieces. Hence, the payroll system you are writing must truncate the actual number of pieces produced to the second digit (i.e., the 10s place).

Review

If the person were being paid per completed batch of ten pieces (rather than per piece), then you would only need to determine the number of completed batches. Since there are 10 pieces per batch, you could accomplish this by dropping the right-most digit. Further, you know from the discussion of digit manipulation in Chapter 3 that this can be accomplished by dividing by 10^1 (using integer division).

For example, letting `number` denote the actual number produced (at full accuracy):

```
batches = number / 10;
```

where `/` denotes integer division. So, an employee that completed 526 pieces completed 52 batches (ignoring the remaining 6 pieces).

Thinking About the Problem

Unfortunately, what you need is not the number of batches but, instead, the number of pieces truncated to the 10s place. Fortunately, given the number of batches, you can calculate this pretty easily. In particular:

```
truncated = batches * 10;
```

So, continuing with the example, the 52 batches corresponds to 520 units truncated to the 10s place.

The Pattern

It turns out that there's nothing special about the 10s place, so the general pattern is easy to see. Letting `place` denote the integer place to truncate to (i.e., `10` for the 10s place, `100` for the 100s place, etc.), then the value truncated to that place is given by:

```
truncated = (number / place) * place;
```

where / again denotes integer division.

One important aspect of this pattern is that it illustrates the importance of not over-generalizing. In particular, at first glance, you might think that the expression `(number / place) * place` could be simplified to `number`. However, this is not the case when using integer division. Specifically, when using integer division, `(a / b) * b` only equals `a` when `a` is evenly divisible by `b`. For example, as discussed above, `(526 / 10) * 10` is equal to `52 * 10` or `520`, which does not equal `526`.

Examples

Suppose you want to talk about something that will happen 87 years after the year 1996. You might want to use the exact year (i.e., `1996 + 87` or `2083`), but you might want to know the decade or century rather than the year. Truncating to the decade (i.e., a `place` of `10`) using the truncation pattern yields `(2083 / 10) * 10` or `208 * 10` or `2080`. Similarly, truncating to the century (i.e., a `place` of `100`) using the truncation pattern yields `(2083 / 100) * 100` or `20 * 10` or `2000`.

Some Warnings

It's important to note that people use the word "truncation" in a variety of different, but related, ways. Most importantly, people often talk about truncating floating point values to integer values (e.g., truncating `3.14` to `3`), which is commonly accomplished using a *type cast* (e.g., `(int)3.14` evaluates to `3`). Our concern here is with a different notion of truncation.

It's also important to distinguish between the accuracy used when performing calculations and the accuracy (or format) used when displaying output. In some situations it is necessary to perform calculations using truncated values. In other situations it is necessary to perform calculations using all of the digits of accuracy available and truncate at the end. In still other situations it is necessary to perform calculations using all of the digits of accuracy available and then format the output when it is displayed. It is your responsibility to know what is required of a particular section of code.

[PART II]

Patterns Requiring Knowledge of Logical and Relational Operators, Conditions, and Methods

Part II contains programming patterns that require an understanding of logical operators, relational operators, conditions, and methods. Specifically, this part of the book contains the following programming patterns:

Indicators. Solutions to problems in which a binary variable is used to determine whether or not another variable should be increased/decreased by an amount/percentage.

Indicator Methods. Solutions to problems in which an indicator must be calculated before it can be used.

Rounding. Solutions to the problem of rounding (rather than truncating) an integer to a particular digit (i.e., power of 10).

Starts and Completions. Solutions to problems that require the number of tasks started and/or completed given a measure of work and an amount of work per task.

Bit Flags. Solutions to problems in which the flow of a

program needs to be controlled based on the state of one or more binary values.

Digit Counting. A solution to the problem of determining the number of digits in an integer.

Some of the patterns in this part of the book don't make direct use of the prerequisite concepts but alternative solutions do. This is true, for example, of indicators. Some of the patterns in this part of the book make direct use of only some of of the prerequisite concepts (e.g., bit flags make use of relational operators and digit counting makes use of methods). Other patterns in this part of the books make direct use of all of the prerequisite concepts (e.g., indicator methods, rounding, and starts and completions). Hence, you may be able to understand some of these patterns before you have learned about all of the prerequisite concepts.

It's also important to note that many of the patterns in this part of the book make use of patterns from earlier in the book. Hence, it is important to understand the patterns from Part I before starting on Part II.

Finally, some of the patterns in this part of the book can be thought of as specific examples of a more abstract pattern. However, that view requires a level of sophistication that beginning programmers may not have, so they are not presented in that way.

[6]

Indicators

Many programs must perform calculations that vary based on conditions of one kind or another. There are many different ways to accomplish this but one very powerful (and common) solution is to use a multiplicative variable that takes on the value zero when the condition isn't satisfied and the value one when it is.

Motivation

Variables of this kind are common in many branches of mathematics and are called *indicator variables.*[1] They are often denoted using a lowercase delta (i.e., δ)[2], often with a subscript to denote the condition (e.g., δ_s to indicate whether a person smokes or not). Indicator variables are then multiplied by other variables in more complex expressions.

For example, suppose you are writing a program to predict the birth weight of babies (in grams) from the gestation period (in weeks). You might theorize that the weight will be lower if the mother smokes during pregnancy. Ignoring whether the mother did or didn't smoke, after collecting data from a

1. In statistics, they are sometimes called *dummy variables.*
2. Don't confuse this with an uppercase delta (i.e., Δ) that is often used to denote a change.

(random or representative) sample of the population, you might determine a relationship like the following:

$$w = -2200 + 148.2g$$

where w (the *dependent variable*) denotes the birth weight (in grams), and g (an *independent variable*) denotes the gestation period (in weeks).[3] Accounting for the mother's smoking behavior, you might determine that the birth weight was, on average, 238.6 grams lower when the mother smoked. You now need to decide how to account for this in your program.

Thinking About The Problem

What you want to do is lower w when the mother smoked and leave w unchanged when the mother didn't smoke. Since there are only two possible states (i.e., the mother smoked or didn't), you might be tempted to use a `boolean` variable to keep track of this information. However, it turns out that it is better to use a discrete variable that is assigned either `0` or `1`, rather than one that takes on the values `true` or `false`. The reason is that you can use a numeric variable with the multiplication operator, and you can't do so with a `boolean` variable. In other words, a `boolean` variable can't be either the right-side or the left-side operand of the multiplication operator.

In particular, suppose you add another independent variable, δ_s, and assign the value 1 to δ_s if the mother smoked during pregnancy and assign the value 0 to δ_s otherwise. Then, the equation for w can be expressed succinctly as follows:

$$w = -2200 + 148.2g - 238.6\delta_s$$

In this way, w will be reduced by 238.6 when δ_s is 1 and will be left unchanged when δ_s is 0.

Note that you could define the indicator variable differently. Specifically, you could assign 1 to δ_s if the mother **didn't smoke** during pregnancy and assign 0 to it otherwise. In this case, the equation for w would be

3. Don't be confused by the negative constant term. This model is only appropriate for longer gestation periods, in which cases the birth weight will be positive.

$w = -2438.6 + 148.2g + 238.6\delta_s$ (i.e., the constant would change and the sign of the last term would be reversed). The two indicators are called *converses* of each other.

The Pattern

In the simplest cases, all you need to do to use this pattern is to define an `int` variable, assign `0` or `1` to it as appropriate, and then use it multiplicatively in an expression.[4] In more complicated cases, you may need multiple indicators, each with its own multiplier.

The converse indicator must take on the value `1` when the original indicator takes on the value `0`, and vice versa. This can be accomplished by subtracting the original indicator's value from `1` and assigning the result to the converse indicator. In other words, the converse indicator is simply 1 minus the original indicator. Which is the "original" and which is the "converse" is completely arbitrary.

This idea can be expressed as the following pattern:

```
total = base + (indicator * adjustment);
```

with the converse indicator given by:

```
converse = 1 - indicator;
```

Examples

Returning to the birth weight example, the code for calculating the weight can be implemented as follows:

```
w = -2200.0 + (148.2 * g) - (238.6 * delta_s);
```

where `w` contains the weight, `g` contains the gestation period, and `delta_s` contains the value `1` if the mother smoked and `0` otherwise.[5] Initializing `g` to the average gestation period of `40.0`

4. You can also use a `double` variable for the indicator if the indicator is to be multiplied by a `double` variable. However, this is a situation in which most people agree that it is appropriate to use an `int` and *type promotion*.
5. In programming languages that allow them in identifiers, it is common to use the underscore character to indicate a subscript.

weeks, you could then use the statement to compare the birth weights for the two possible values of `delta_s`. A `delta_s` of `0` would result in a birth weight of `3728.0` while a `delta_s` of `1` would result in a birth weight of `3489.4`.

As another example, suppose the fine associated with a first parking ticket is smaller than the fine associated with subsequent parking tickets (specifically, $10.00 for the first ticket and $45.00 for subsequent tickets). In this case, if you assign `0` to `ticketedIndicator` when the person has no prior parking tickets and assign `1` to it otherwise, then you can write the statement to calculate the fine as follows.

```
baseFine = 10.00;
repeatOffenderPenalty = 35.00;
totalFine = baseFine + (ticketedIndicator * repeatOffenderPenalty);
```

As a final example, consider a rental car company that charges a base rate of $19.95 per day. There is a surcharge of $5.00 per day if multiple people drive the car, and a surcharge of $10.00 per day if any driver is under 25 years of age. If you assign `1` to `multiIndicator` when there are multiple drivers and you assign `1` to `youngIndicator` when there are any drivers under 25, then you can write the statement to calculate the rate as follows:

```
baseRate =  19.95;
ageSurcharge =  10.00;
multiSurcharge = 5.00;

rate = baseRate + (multiIndicator * multiSurcharge)
                + (youngIndicator * ageSurcharge);
```

Some Warnings

The descriptions of the examples in this chapter may have led you to use a different solution than the one discussed above. While you may, in the end, prefer such a solution, you should think carefully about the advantages and disadvantages before you make any decisions.

Using `if` Statements

You might be attempted to use a `boolean` variable, `if` statement, and the updating pattern from Chapter 1 rather than an indicator, and there are times when this is appropriate. However, in general, indicators are much less verbose.

For example, returning to the birth weight problem, if you assign `true` to `smoker` when the mother smoked during the pregnancy, then you can calculate the birth weight as follows:

```
w = -2200.0 + (148.2 * g);
if (smoker) {
    w -= 238.6;
}
```

This solution is much less concise than the solution that uses indicator variables. It also treats the continuous independent variable (g in this case) and the discrete independent variable (δ_s in this case) differently, for no apparent reason.

This approach gets even more verbose as the number of discrete independent variables increases. For example, returning to the car rental problem, if you assign `true` to `areMultipleDrivers` when there are multiple drivers and you assign `true` to `areYoung` when there are any drivers under 25, then you can calculate the rental rate as follows:

```
baseRate =  19.95;
ageSurcharge =  10.00;
multiSurcharge = 5.00;

rate = baseRate;
if (areMultipleDrivers) {
    rate += multiSurcharge;
}
if (areYoung) {
    rate += ageSurcharge;
}
```

When using indicator variables, each additional discrete independent variable only leads to an additional term in the single assignment statement. When using `boolean` variables, each additional discrete independent variable leads to an additional `if` statement.

Using Ternary Operators

You might also be tempted to use a `boolean` variable, the ternary conditional operator, and the updating pattern from Chapter 1 rather than an indicator, but this is almost never appropriate. For example, returning to the parking ticket problem, if you assign the value `true` to the `boolean` variable `hasBeenTicketed` when the person has a previous ticket, then you can calculate the total fine as follows:

```
baseFine = 10.00;
repeatOffenderPenalty = 35.00;
totalFine = hasBeenTicketed ? baseFine + repeatOffenderPenalty : baseFine;
```

Some people do prefer this solution to the one that uses an `if` for stylistic reasons. That is, they think the ternary conditional operator is more concise. However, it is not more concise than the solution that uses an indicator variable, so it is hard to argue that it should be preferred.

Further, when the number of discrete independent variables increases this approach gets much less concise. Returning to the car rental problem you could calculate the rental rate as follows:

```
baseRate =  19.95;
ageSurcharge =  10.00;
multiSurcharge = 5.00;
rate = areMultipleDrivers ? baseRate + multiSurcharge +
     (areYoung ? ageSurcharge : 0.0) : baseRate +
     (areYoung ? ageSurcharge : 0.0);
```

However, this statement is very verbose (and, many people think, difficult to understand).

You could, instead, calculate the rental rate as follows:

```
baseRate =  19.95;
ageSurcharge =  10.00;
multiSurcharge = 5.00;

rate = baseRate;
rate += areMultipleDrivers ? multiSurcharge : 0;
rate += areYoung ? ageSurcharge : 0;
```

Again, while some people may prefer this solution to the one that uses `if` statements because it is more concise, it is less concise than the solution that uses indicator variables.

[7]

Indicator Methods

Sometimes the value needed to perform a calculation is known, and other times it too must be calculated. This is true of both "traditional" values and indicators (of the kind discussed in Chapter 6). This chapter considers problems in which an indicator's value must be calculated before it can be used in another expression.

Motivation

There's a famous saying among performers, "the show must go on", which means that there must be a show whenever there's an audience. In the context of Chapter 6 on indicators, this means that the number of seats sold for a particular showtime must be used to calculate an indicator, setting it to `0` when no tickets have been sold and setting it to `1` otherwise. This is an example of a *threshold indicator* in which the threshold is 1.

So, given that some number of tickets has been sold for a particular show time, you must determine the number of shows that must be offered at that time (i.e., either `0` or `1`). Letting `shows` denote the number of shows and `sold` denote the number of tickets sold, you want to calculate `shows` from `sold` in such a way that it takes on the value `0` when `sold` is 0 and it takes on the value `1` for all positive values of `sold`.

Review

You could, of course, calculate the value of the variable shows as follows:

```
if (sold >= 1) {
    shows = 1;
} else {
    shows = 0;
}
```

However, you should also know that this is a bad practice, since it is likely that you will need to use this simple algorithm in more than one place. Hence, to avoid code duplication, you should instead write a method like the following:

```
public static int shows(int sold) {
    if (sold >= 1) {
        return 1;
    } else {
        return 0;
    }
}
```

and use it as needed.

The Pattern

The entertainment example is, obviously, a very particular problem. However, it can easily be generalized to uncover a pattern. In particular, the entertainment problem is a particular example of a general problem in which you need to determine whether a particular value exceeds a particular threshold. Further, there is an even more general problem in which you need a method that returns a value of 0 or 1 based on the value of the parameters it is passed.

For threshold indicators, the solution to the problem is the following method:

```
public static int indicator(int value, int threshold) {
    if (value >= threshold) {
        return 1;
    } else {
        return 0;
    }
}
```

For other indicators, the solution is a method with parameters that vary with the specifics of the problem.

Examples

It's useful to consider examples of both threshold indicators and other indicators.

Threshold Indicators

Continuing with the entertainment example, the threshold is `1` (i.e., if the size of the audience is 1 or more then there must be a show), so given the size of the audience (represented by the variable `size`), the number of shows is given by the following:

```
shows = indicator(sold, 1);
```

Returning to the parking ticket example used in Chapter 6, letting the number of prior tickets be given by `priors`, the fine can be calculated as follows:

```
baseFine = 10.00;
repeatOffenderPenalty = 35.00;
totalFine = baseFine + (indicator(priors, 1) * repeatOffenderPenalty);
```

It is also instructive to return to the car rental example from Chapter 6. For this example, you can initialize the necessary variables as follows:

```
baseRate = 19.95;
ageSurcharge = 10.00;
ageThreshold = 25;
multiSurcharge = 5.00;
multiThreshold = 1;
```

Then, you can calculate the daily rental rate as follows:

```
rate = baseRate
    + (1 - indicator(minimumAge, ageThreshold)) * ageSurcharge
    + indicator(extraDrivers, multiThreshold) * multiSurcharge;
```

Notice that, the age surcharge uses a converse threshold indicator while the multi-driver surcharge uses an ordinary threshold indicator.

Other Indicators

As an example of a more general indicator, consider the following method for calculating a person's basic metabolic rate (BMR):

$$b = 5.00 + 10.00m + 6.25h - 5.00a - 161.00\delta_f$$

where b denotes the BMR (in kilocalories per day), m denotes the person's mass (in kilograms), h denotes the person's height (in centimeters), a denotes the person's age (in years), and δ_f is 1 if the person is female and 0 otherwise.

Now, suppose the `double` variables `m`, `h`, and `a` contain the values of the person's mass, height, and age (respectively), and the `String` variable `s` contains the person's sex. Then, you would create the following indicator method:

```
public static int indicator(char sex) {
    if ((sex == 'F') || (sex == 'f')) {
        return 1;
    } else {
        return 0;
    }
}
```

and use it as follows:

```
    b = 5.00 + 10.00 * m + 6.35 * h - 5.00 * a - 161.00 * indicator(s);
```

Some Warnings

As in the discussion of indicator variables in Chapter 6, you might think that you should use `boolean` variables, `if` statements, and the updating pattern from Chapter 1 instead of indicator methods. The trade-offs here are the same as the trade-offs there.

It is also important to realize that you shouldn't over-generalize the code that is used in this pattern. Suppose, for example, you needed to assign the value `true` to the `boolean` variable `isLegal` if and only if the value in the variable `age` is greater than or equal to the value in the "constant" `DRINKING_AGE`. Given the code used to implement the pattern, you might be tempted to do something like the following.

```
if (age >= DRINKING_AGE) {
    isLegal = true;
} else {
    isLegal = false;
}
```

However, most people think this is completely inappropriate (and demonstrates a lack of understanding of relational operators and `boolean` variables). Instead, it should be implemented as follows:

```
isLegal = (age >= DRINKING_AGE);
```

That is, the expression `(age >= DRINKING_AGE)` evaluates to a `boolean` that should be directly assigned to the variable `isLegal` — the `if` statement is superfluous. In other words, a pattern that is appropriate for assigning values to numeric variables or returning numeric values (like those in the previous section) may not be appropriate for `boolean` variables.

Looking Ahead

On some hardware architectures, `if` statements (including the `boolean` expressions that must be evaluated) take more CPU time to execute than arithmetic operations. Hence, on such architectures it is important to replace `if` statements with arithmetic expressions. Threshold indicators are an example of this that might arise in a course on computer architecture.

If you've read Chapter 4 on arithmetic on the circle, you're may be thinking about how you can use the integer division operator and/or the remainder operator to eliminate the `if` statements. While it is, indeed, possible to do so, the solution is not obvious. Consider the following candidates:

- `(value / (max + 1))` is `0` when `value` is `0`, it is also `0` for every other possible `int`.
- `(value / max)` is slightly better since it is `0` when `value` is `0`, and `1` when `value` is `max`, but it is still `0` for every other possible `int`.
- `value % (max + 1)` is `0` when `value` is `0`, and is `1` when `value` is `1`, it is `value` (not `1`) otherwise. (Using `max` rather than `(max + 1)` in the denominator does not

improve things.)

The easiest way to think about a solution that does work is to consider the problem in three stages. First, consider the case when the threshold is less than twice the value. Then, consider the special case of a non-zero threshold indicator (i.e., when the threshold is 1). Finally, consider the general case (i.e., the threshold can be anything).

A Threshold Less Than Twice the Value

When `value` is strictly less than `(2 * threshold)`, it follows that `(value / threshold)` is going to be either `0` or `1` (because, using real division, the result will always be less than `2`). Hence, in this case, you can find the `indicator` as follows:

```
indicator = (value / threshold);
```

Unfortunately, this won't work in general because we don't always know `value`.

A Threshold of 1

One way to get to the correct solution to the special case when the threshold is `1` is to find `max` consecutive integers that have the property that each divided by some value is `1`.

To move in the right direction, observe that for `value` in the set **{1, 2, ..., max}** it follows that `(value + max)` is an element of the set **{(1+max), (2+max), ..., (value+max)}**. Since `value` is less than or equal to `max`, it also follows that each element of this set is less than or equal to `(2*max)`. Hence, the result of dividing each element by `(max+1)` (using integer division) is `1` (because using real division the result would be strictly between `1` and `2`).

To finalize the pattern when the threshold is `1`, observe that `(0 + max) / (max + 1)` is `0` (using integer division), since the numerator is strictly less than the denominator. What this means is that the pattern when the threshold is `1` can be expressed as the following non-zero indicator:

```
indicatorNZ = (value + max) / (max + 1);
```

The General Case

In the general case, you need to create an indicator that is `0` when a non-negative `value` is less some `threshold` and `1` otherwise. The easiest way to create such an indicator is to first calculate an intermediate value that is `0` when the `value` is less than the `threshold` and positive otherwise, and then use a non-zero indicator.

To do so, observe that, since both `value` and `threshold` are in the interval $[\mathtt{0}, \mathtt{max}]$, it follows that, as required, `(value / threshold)` is `0` when `value` is less than `threshold` and that it is in $[\mathtt{1}, \mathtt{max}]$ otherwise. Hence, you can calculate `intermediate` as follows:

```
intermediate = value / threshold;
```

Then, you can use `intermediate` and the expression for a non-zero indicator to calculate a threshold indicator as follows:

```
indicatorT = (intermediate + max) / (max + 1);
```

Putting it all together yields the following general expression for a threshold indicator:

```
indicatorT = ((value / threshold) + max) / (max + 1);
```

To see that this is, indeed, a generalization of the special case, you need only substitute `1` for `threshold` in this expression.

This leads to a general-purpose method like the following for calculating the threshold indicator without an `if` statement:

```
public static int aindicator(int value, int threshold, int max) {
    return ((value / threshold) + max) / (max + 1);
}
```

[8]

Rounding

As mentioned in Chapter 5, integers commonly include more digits of accuracy than needed, and this sometimes leads to the need to truncate numbers. This chapter considers a common alternative to truncation — rounding.

Motivation

In the example from Chapter 5, the worker was paid per piece, but only for multiples of ten pieces. So, the number of pieces manufactured was truncated to the 10s place. Not surprisingly, this policy might make workers unhappy. So, in an effort to improve job satisfaction, the company might decide to round to the 10s place rather than truncate to it.

Review

Under the system in Chapter 5, if an employee manufactured 526 items then they would be paid for 520 items. As you now know, letting `number` denote the value of interest and `place` denote the place to truncate to (e.g., 10, 100, 1000, etc.), you can calculate the truncated value using the following pattern:

```
truncated = (number / place) * place;
```

Thinking About The Problem

Given the original value and the truncated value, it shouldn't be too difficult to find the rounded value. All that's needed is a way to determine if the rounded value is larger than the truncated value or not. If it is, then an appropriate adjustment must be added to the truncated value.

Returning to the manufacturing example, the truncated value is 520. What about the rounded value? Since the actual number of items is 526, and 526 is at least halfway between 520 and 530, the rounded value should be 530. Hence, the truncated value needs to be adjusted by 10 to get the rounded value.

Going from this specific example to a more general solution requires two observations. First, if the rounded value is larger than the truncated value, it is larger by exactly the amount `place` (i.e., 10 in the example). Second, to determine if the rounded value should be larger than the truncated value, you need to compare the difference between the number and the truncated value (i.e., 6 in the example), which is also the remainder after division with **half of** the amount `place`.

The Pattern

So, given the truncated value as calculated above, you can calculate the rounded value as follows:

```
if ((number % place) >= (place / 2)) {
    rounded = truncated + place;
} else {
    rounded = truncated;
}
```

Note that, since `place` will always be a power of ten, no complications arise when dividing it (an integer) by `2` (another integer). In other words, `place` is always evenly divisible by `2`.

Putting it all together, you can write a method like the following for solving general rounding problems.

```
public static int round(int number, int place) {
    int rounded, truncated;

    truncated = (number / place) * place;

    if ((number % place) >= (place / 2)) {
```

```
        rounded = truncated + place;
    } else {
        rounded = truncated;
    }

    return rounded;
}
```

In essence, this pattern is a combination of the truncation pattern from Chapter 5 and a threshold indicator from Chapter 6. It is also a good example of how patterns can be combined to solve other problems.

Examples

Returning to the manufacturing example, given an `int` variable named `items`, you can determine how much an employee that produces `526` items should be paid by calculating the rounded number of items as follows:

```
items = 526;
place = 10;
rounded = round(items, place);
```

As another example, suppose you want to talk about something that will happen 93 years after the year 1993. You might want to be exact and use the year 2086, but you also might want to round to the nearest decade or century. Using the rounding pattern, this can be accomplished as follows:

```
exact   = (1993 + 93);
decade  = round(exact,  10);
century = round(exact, 100);
```

In the first invocation, the value of `truncated` will be `2080`, the value of `number % place` will be `6` (which is greater than `place / 2` which is `5`), so the value of `rounded` will be `2090`. In the second invocation, the value of `truncated` will be `2000`, the value of `number % place` will be `86` (which is greater than `place / 2` which is `50`), so the value of `rounded` will be `2100`.

A Warning

As mentioned in Chapter 5 on the truncation pattern, it is important to distinguish between the numerical accuracy that should be used when performing calculations and the accuracy (or format) used when displaying output. It is your responsibility to know what is required of a particular section of code.

Looking Ahead

As mentioned in Chapter 7 in the discussion of threshold indicators, on some kinds of hardware, these kinds of calculations sometimes need to be performed using arithmetic operators only (i.e., without the use of `if` statements). Fortunately, doing so is not very difficult. To understand how, it is easiest to build up to the general case from some specific cases.

If you need to round to the 10s place then you need to know if the remainder is greater than or equal to the threshold of 5, in which case you should increase the truncated value by 10. Otherwise, you shouldn't increase it (or you should increase it by 0). In this case, since `remainder % 5` is 1 when `remainder` is greater than or equal to the threshold of 5 and is 0 otherwise, you can write the increase as:

```
increase = (remainder % 5) * 10;
```

If you need to round to the 100s place, however, things are a little more complicated because then the question is not whether the remainder is greater than or equal to 5, but whether the remainder is greater than or equal to the threshold of 50. This means that, if the threshold is calculated as follows:

```
threshold = 5 * (100 / 10);
```

then `threshold` is less than `2 * value`, and you can use the simplest arithmetic threshold indicator from Chapter 7. In particular:

```
indicator = remainder / threshold;
```

You can then calculate the increase as follows.

```
increase = indicator * 100;
```

Letting `place` denote the place being rounded to (i.e., `10` for the

10s place, `100` for the 100s place, etc.) this can be generalized as follows:

```
truncated = number / place;
remainder = number % place;
threshold = 5 * (place / 10);
indicator = remainder / threshold;
increase = indicator * place;
rounded = truncated + increase;
```

where all of the variables are integers.

[9]

Starts and Completions

Programs frequently need to determine the number of tasks associated with an amount of work, given a measure of the amount of work per task. Sometimes the need is for the number of tasks that were started, and sometimes the need is for the number of tasks completed. This chapter considers solutions to these kinds of problems.

Motivation

The terminology used in the name of this pattern comes from baseball/softball, where it is common to track the number of times a pitcher starts a game and the number of times that they complete that same game. However, as a motivating example, it is better to think about running. For example, suppose you are working for a charity that has organized a fund raising event in which donations are tied to the integer number of laps (started or completed, depending on the donor) rather than the number of miles. Each participant has a wrist band that tracks the number of miles they run. Your job is to write a program that calculates the number of laps that a runner has started and completed given the number of miles run (the measure of work) and the number of miles per lap (the amount of work per task).

Thinking About the Problem

The naive approach to finding the number of completions is to use division. For example, if a participant has run 7 miles over a 3 mile track, then they have run $7/3 = 2\frac{1}{3}$ laps. The obvious shortcoming of this approach is that the result isn't an integer and donations are promised per "whole" lap.

Fortunately, you know how to solve this problem. In fact, the example itself should bring to mind the notion of doing arithmetic on a circle (or, an oval, in this case) and the use of integer division. It then follows that `0` miles corresponds to `0/3` (i.e. `0`) laps, `1` mile corresponds to `1/3` (i.e., `0`) laps, `7` miles corresponds to `7/3` (i.e. `2` laps), `9` miles corresponds to `9/3` (i.e., `3`) laps, etc.

Given this observation, you might then think that all you need to do to find the number of starts is to add one to the number of completions, and a few tests might convince you that this is, indeed, the case. For example, `7` miles over a `3` mile track corresponds to `7/3` (i.e. `2`) completions and `7/3 + 1` (i.e., `3`) starts. Unfortunately, this "solution" is only correct for some cases. For example, `9` miles over a `3` mile track corresponds to `3` completions and `3` starts (**not** `4` starts). In other words, in general, you should only add `1` to the number of completions when the denominator isn't evenly divisible by the numerator.

The Pattern

The simple part of the pattern involves ideas from Chapter 4 on arithmetic on the circle and can be written as:

```
public static int completions(int work, int workPerTask) {
    return work / workPerTask;
}
```

where `work` would correspond to the number of miles run and `workPerTask` would correspond to the length of the track.

The more complicated part of the pattern, on the other hand, involves an indicator method from Chapter 7, and is given by:

```
public static int starts(int work, int workPerTask) {
```

```
        return completions(work, workPerTask)
            + remainderIndicator(work, workPerTask);
    }
```

where `remainderIndicator()` is `1` when any "extra" miles have been run and is `0` otherwise. In other words, `remainderIndicator()` is given by:

```
public static int remainderIndicator(int num, int den) {
    if ((num % den) == 0) {
        return 0;
    } else {
        return 1;
    }
}
```

Examples

As an example, suppose a very energetic participant in the charity event runs 26 miles (just short of a marathon). Then, that person completed `8` laps (i.e., `26 / 3`), but started `9` (since `26 % 3` is non-zero).

As another example, suppose a starting pitcher works for `7` innings in a baseball game (that is `9` innings long). Then, that pitcher did not complete the game (since `completions(7, 9)` is `0`) but did start the game (since `completions(7, 9) + remainderIndicator(7, 9)` is `1`). On the other hand, a starting pitcher that works all `9` innings has `1` (i.e., `9 / 9`) completion and `1` start (since `9 % 9` is `0`).

Looking Ahead

As mentioned briefly in Chapter 7, you may take advanced courses that consider situations in which it is important to avoid the use of `if` statements. There are two different ways to accomplish this when solving starts and completions problems.

An Arithmetic Solution

One approach is to use a threshold indicator instead of the indicator method used above. In this context, `(miles % length)` (the number of "extra" miles run) plays the role of `value`, and `length` plays the role of `max`. What this means is that the `indicator` is given by:

```
indicator = ((miles % length) + length) / (length + 1);
```

Putting it all together, `starts` is given by:

```
starts = (miles / length)
    + (((miles % length) + length) / (length + 1));
```

An Alternative Arithmetic Solution

Integer division can be defined in two different ways, an idea that is often discussed in great detail in upper level courses. For now, you can get some understanding of this idea by considering a different way of solving the starts problem.

To begin, ignore situations in which the numerator is 0. Then, considering an example in which the number of miles is between `1` and `6` (inclusive), the complete set of numerators is given by $\{1, 2, 3, 4, 5, 6\}$. If you simply divide (using integer division) each of these elements by the denominator `3` (i.e., the length of the track in miles), you get the set $\{0, 0, 1, 1, 1, 2\}$, which is clearly incorrect.

But, maybe the mistake is because you've started counting from 1 instead of from 0. So, you start from 0 instead. In this case, the set of numerators is $\{0, 1, 2, 3, 4, 5\}$. If you now divide (again using integer division) each of these elements by the denominator `3`, you get the set $\{0, 0, 0, 1, 1, 1\}$. Now, each element of the set is only off by `1`. So, you only need to add `1` to the result of the integer division to get the correct answer.

In other words, ignoring situations in which `miles` is `0` you have the following:

```
starts = ((miles - 1) / length) + 1;
```

Now you need to consider whether this solution will work when the numerator is `0`, which depends entirely on what `-1 / length` evaluates to. It turns out that there are two possible answers, depending on how integer division is defined.

In one definition, the result of an integer division is moved towards 0. Using this definition, `-1 / length` evaluates to `0`. This is the way integer division using the `/` operator works in Java. Using this definition of integer division, the alternative solution

does not work when `miles` is `0` (because the result should be `0` but will be `1`).

In the other definition, the result of an integer division is moved towards negative infinity. Using this definition, `-1 / length` evaluates to `-1`. This is the way integer division using the `Math.floorDiv()` method works in Java. Using this definition of integer division, the alternative pattern **does** work when `miles` is `0` (because the result should and will be `0`). In other words, the following solution:

```
starts = Math.floorDiv((miles - 1), length) + 1;
```

does work.

[10]

Bit Flags

The flow of a program is often controlled using one or more *flags*, which are binary values (i.e., yes/no, on/off, true/false) that indicate the current or desired state of the system. This chapter considers one common approach for working with flags.

Motivation

Suppose you're developing an adventure game in which there are a variety of different items that players can collect and put in their inventory, and the actions that players can take (and the results of those actions) depend on the items that they have in their possession. Without knowing anything else about the game, it's clear that the program will include a variety of `if` statements that will control the flow, and that these `if` statements will have `boolean` expressions that involve the variables that represent the items. This chapter will help you solve problems that involve the management of, and the performance of operations on, these kinds of variables.

Review

You could, of course, have a `boolean` variable for each item that is assigned `true` when the player has the item and `false` otherwise. The shortcoming of this approach is that there tends to be a large number of such variables, and they all need to be passed into the various methods that need them.[1]

Thinking About The Problem

Bit flags take advantage of the fact that everything in a digital computer is stored as 0s and 1s. For example, suppose a non-negative integer is represented by 4 bits, each of which can contain a 0 or 1. Each of the 4 positions corresponds to a power of 2 (i.e., the 1s place, the 2s place, the 4s place, and the 8s place). This is illustrated in Figure 10.1 for the 4-bit binary number `1101`, which is 13 in base 10. (If you're confused, see Figure 3.1 for an example that uses base 10.)

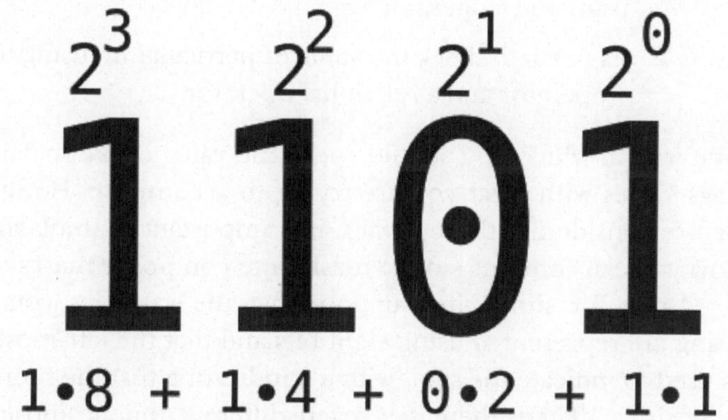

Figure 10.1. Binary Representations of an Integer

Given this representational scheme, you can use a single non-negative 4-bit integer to hold up to four different binary flags. Then, you can use the `&`, `|`, and `^` operators to perform bitwise "and", "inclusive or", and "exclusive or" operations on these integer values.

1. If you already know about arrays, you might think that a `boolean[]` array would resolve this shortcoming. While that's true, it introduces another shortcoming, the need to keep track of the correspondence between index numbers and inventory items.

The Pattern

For simplicity, assume that the number of flags you need to work with can be represented using a single variable (e.g., one `int` or `long`). The pattern then involves several steps:

1. Create *masks* that represent each of the binary states of interest. Each mask is a variable of appropriate type that is initialized to a unique power of 2.
2. Declare a variable that will hold the bit flags.
3. As needed, *set* particular bits (i.e., make the bits 1) using the `|` operator, *clear* particular bits (i.e., make the bits 0) using the `&` operator, and/or *toggle* particular bits (i.e., switch the bits to their other value) using the `^` operator.
4. As needed, check the value of particular bit using the `|` operator and a relational operator.

The way in which you should check the value of particular bit flags varies with what you are trying to accomplish. However, before considering those details, it is important to think about how you can combine simple masks into composite masks.

Again for simplicity, suppose that the variables you are using are represented using eight bits and that the left-most bit is used to indicate the sign (with a `0` indicating that the number is positive). Then, there are seven different unique (positive) masks, as follows: `00000001`, `00000010`, `00000100`, `00001000`, `00010000`, `00100000`, and `01000000`, each of which has a single bit that is set. You can create a composite mask (i.e., a mask with more than one bit set) using the `|` operator. For example, suppose you want a composite mask with both the left-most usable bit and the right-most bit set. You can accomplish this as follows:

```
  00000001
| 01000000
----------
  01000001
```

Now, suppose you have a composite mask named `needed`

and a state variable named `actual`. There are several things you might want to know about the relationship between the two, and each question must be answered slightly differently.

Suppose you want to know if **any** of the bits that are set in `needed` are also set in `actual`. You can accomplish this as follows:

```
public static boolean anyOf(int needed, int actual) {
    return (needed & actual) > 0;
}
```

The expression `needed & actual` evaluates to a value in which a particular bit in that value is set if and only if the corresponding bit is set in both `needed` and `actual`. Then, if any bit in `needed & actual` is set, the expression `(needed & actual) > 0` will evaluate to `true`.

Instead, you might want to know if **all** of the bits that are set in `needed` are also set in `actual`. You can accomplish this as follows:

```
public static boolean allOf(int needed, int actual) {
    return (needed & actual) == needed;
}
```

Finally, you might want to know if **exactly the same** bits in `needed` and `actual` are set. This can be accomplished as follows:

```
public static boolean onlyOf(int needed, int actual) {
    return (needed == actual);
}
```

That is, `needed` and `actual` must be identical.

Examples

Returning to the example of the adventure game, you can represent the individual items using the following masks:

```
public static final int FOOD   =  1;
public static final int SPELL  =  2;
public static final int POTION =  4;
public static final int WAND   =  8;
public static final int WATER  = 16;
// And so on...
```

You can then represent the player's inventory as a single `int` as follows:

```
int inventory;
inventory = 0;
```

When the player acquires an individual item, you can use the bitwise "or" operator to adjust the `inventory`. For example, suppose the player acquires `WATER`. You can use the updating pattern from Chapter 1 as follows:

```
inventory = inventory | WATER;
```

At this point, the variable `inventory` contains the value `16`. But, what's important is that the bit corresponding to "having water" is set.

Suppose the player later acquires `SPELL`. You can handle this as follows (using the compound assignment operator in this case, to illustrate its use):

```
inventory |= SPELL;
```

At this point, the variable `inventory` contains the value `18`. But, again, what's important is that the bits corresponding to "having spell" and "having water" are set.

You can then check to see if the bit corresponding to "having water" is set as follows:

```
boolean haveWater = (inventory & WATER) > 0;
```

Note that either the `allOf()` algorithm or the `anyOf()` algorithm would work in this case, since the mask is not composite.

Similarly, you can then check to see if the bit corresponding to "having a potion" is set as follows:

```
boolean havePotion = (inventory & POTION) > 0;
```

When the player later drinks the water, you can clear that bit as follows:

```
inventory = inventory & (WATER ^ Integer.MAX_VALUE);
```

Here, since `Integer.MAX_VALUE` is an `int` in which every bit is 1 (except for the sign bit), the result of `(WATER ^ Integer.MAX_VALUE)` is a mask in which all of the bits of `WATER` (except the sign bit) have been toggled. This is easy to see using 8-bit `int` values as follows:

```
  00010000
^ 01111111
----------
  01101111
```

So, since the bit that corresponds to water in this new mask is 0, The bitwise `&` of `inventory` with this new mask will clear the bit that corresponds to water in the result.

Some Warnings

Note that beginning programmers commonly use the wrong bitwise operator when creating composite masks. This is because they tend to describe the process as setting one bit **and** another bit. However, if you take the bitwise `&` of two simple masks, the result will always be zero. For example, consider the 8-bit representations of the mask for food and the mask for water. Suppose you want to create a composite mask to determine if the player has both food and water. If you create the mask using the bitwise `&` operator, you get the following:

```
  00000001
& 00010000
----------
  00000000
```

If, instead, you use the bitwise `|` operator, you get the desired result, as follows:

```
  00000001
| 00010000
----------
  00010001
```

Note that beginning programmers also make the same mistake when updating the variable that contains the current state. Again, using 8-bit representations, suppose the player has water. Then `inventory` will be `00010000`. When the player later acquires the spell, you must use the bitwise `|` operator as follows:

```
  00010000
| 00000010
----------
  00010010
```

If you used the bitwise `&` operator (thinking the player has water **and** the spell), you would wind up with nothing in `inventory`. This can be shown as follows:

```
  00010000
& 00000010
----------
  00000000
```

Looking Ahead

At this point, it is sufficient to think that integer values are represented in a specified number of bits with the left-most bit indicating the sign (`0` for positive values and `1` for negative values). In fact, this is not the representational scheme that is used most commonly. One easily understood problem with such a scheme is that there are two different representations of zero. Using eight bits, this scheme has both positive zero (i.e., `00000000`) and negative zero (i.e., `10000000`). When you take a deeper look at data types, you will learn that the most common representation of integers is a system called *two's complement*. This system works essentially like an odometer, with a single zero (i.e., `00000000`) that rolls up to the first positive integer (i.e., `00000001`) and rolls back to the first negative integer (i.e., `11111111`). This means that there is one more negative number than there are positive numbers. Fortunately, the left-most bit of all negative numbers is still `1` and the left-most bit of all positive numbers is still `0`.

If, in the future, you take a course on data structures and algorithms you may also learn about the `BitSet` class which allows the number of flags to "grow". In particular, you may consider the time and space efficiency of providing this functionality.

[11]

Digit Counting

There are many situations in which a program needs to know the number of digits in an `int`. Unfortunately, `int` variables don't have properties other than their value. In other words, anthropomorphizing a little, `int` variables don't know anything about themselves. This chapter considers solutions to this problem given this observation.

Motivation

As you know from Chapter 3 on digit manipulation, in order to drop or extract digits from the left side of an integer, you needed to know the number of digits in the number. In the examples in that chapter, the number of digits was known. Unfortunately, that isn't always the case. For example, credit card account numbers might have between six and nine digits. The problem, then, is that of determining the number of digits in a number.

Review

As you also know from Chapter 3 on digit manipulation, the position of a digit corresponds to a particular power of 10. Specifically, the digit in position n (counting from the right, **starting with 0**) corresponds to the 10^ns place. For example, position 2 corresponds to the 10^2 or 100s place. To count digits you need to be able to invert the process. For example, to count a three-digit number, you need to find the position that the 100s place corresponds to.

As you hopefully recall, this is the domain of the *logarithm.* In a decimal (i.e., base 10) representation, the $\log_{10}(x)$ is often described as the value of n that 10 must be raised to in order to get x. More formally, $\log_{10}(x)$ is the value of n that satisfies $x = 10^n$. So, returning to our example, the position of the 100s place corresponds to $\log_{10}(100)$, which is 2 (since 10^2 is 100). More generally, $\log_b(x)$ is the value of n that satisfies $x = b^n$, where b is referred to as the base (or *radix*) of the logarithm.

Thinking About The Problem

Evaluating $\log_{10}(x)$ can be quite difficult, in general. However, it is easy to find bounds. For example, since $\log_{10}(100)$ is 2 and $\log_{10}(1000)$ is 3 (and logarithms are monotonic) it follows that $\log_{10}(x)$ is in the interval $[2, 3)$ for any $x \in [100, 1000)$. This means that the $\log_{10}$ of any three-digit number is in $[2, 3)$ and that the $\log_{10}$ of any four-digit number is in $[3, 4)$. For example:

- `Math.log10(7198)` evaluates to approximately `3.8572118423168926` which, as expected, is in the interval $[3, 4)$.
- `Math.log10(462)` evaluates to approximately `2.6646419755561257` which, as expected, is in the interval $[2, 3)$.
- `Math.log10(10000)` evaluates to `5.0` which, as expected, is in the interval $[5, 6)$.

The Pattern

More generally, the $\log_{10}$ of any n-digit number will be in the interval $[n-1, n)$, which means it will be greater than or equal to $n-1$ and strictly less than n. Hence, the integer part of $\log_{10}$ of any n-digit number will be $n-1$. So, the number of digits in the number x is given by:

```
public static int digits(int x) {
    return (int) Math.log10(x) + 1;
}
```

Examples

Returning to the credit card example, suppose that the account number is as follows:

```
    cardNumber = 412831758;
```

Then, you can find the number of digits in the account number as follows:

```
    n = digits(cardNumber);
```

Now, as you know from Chapter 3, if you want to extract the left-most three digits (i.e., the issuer), you need to drop the rightmost `n - 3` digits. This involves dividing by ten to the power of `n-3`, which you can implement as follows:

```
    issuer = cardNumber / (int) Math.pow(10.0, n - 3);
```

As another example, suppose you need to write a program for a newspaper that converts a dollar amount (e.g., a person's annual income, the price of a house) into a phrase like "6 figures" or "7 figures". You would again need to calculate the number of digits in the number of interest. So, for example, if you initialize the variable containing the annual income of the subject of the story as follows:

```
    income = 156720;
```

you can then figure out the number of "figures" in that variable as follows:

```
    figures = digits(income);
```

Looking Ahead

As with the digit manipulation pattern of Chapter 3, this pattern can be used with other representation schemes (i.e., other bases). All that is needed is to replace 10 with the desired base, b.

Fortunately, it is easy to calculate the logarithm in one base given the logarithm in another. That is, assuming you have the ability to calculate $\log_{10}(x)$ (e.g., using `Math.log10()` in Java):

$$\log_a(x) = \frac{\log_{10}(x)}{\log_{10}(a)}$$

whenever $x > 0$.

A Warning

Notice that the truncation pattern from Chapter 5 is **not** used in this pattern. Instead, typecasting is used to get the integer part of the value returned by `Math.log10()`. This is because `Math.log10()` returns a `double`, and the truncation pattern is for truncating integers.

[PART III]

Patterns Requiring Knowledge of Loops, Arrays, and I/O

Part III contains programming patterns that require an understanding of loops/iteration, one-dimensional arrays, and console input/output. Specifically, this part of the book contains the following programming patterns:

Reprompting. Solutions to the problem of prompting a user for input until they provide a valid response.

Accumulators. Solutions to problems that require one (or a few) "running" calculations.

Accumulator Arrays. Solutions to problems that require multiple, related "running" calculations.

Lookup Arrays. Solutions to problems that involve finding the values associated with a key, when the key has special properties.

Interval Membership. A solution to problems that involve finding the interval that contains a particular value.

Conformal Arrays. A solution to the problem of organizing multiple pieces of information that all have a common key.

Segmented Arrays. A solution to the problem of organizing multiple pieces of information of the same type.

Lookup arrays and the interval membership pattern both use arrays in less-than-obvious ways to solve problems of various kinds. They are interesting in their own right, because they help you think about novel ways to use arrays. Conformal arrays and segmented arrays are ways to organize data using arrays and then process the data using loops. They are used quite commonly in languages that don't support object-oriented programming, and, as a result, they often find their way into programs written in object-oriented languages. They also provide an interesting contrast to objects/classes, which can also be used to solve problems of this kind.

[12]

Reprompting

Programs that use the console (sometimes called command-line programs) frequently need to prompt the user to provide input, validate the input, and reprompt if the input is invalid. There are many different ways to accomplish these tasks, but, as with all of the problems discussed thus far, there are better and worse ways to do so.

Motivation

Suppose you must write a program that prompts the user to enter their age and then retrieves their response. Since the user might make a mistake and enter a negative value, your program must check the user's response and reprompt them if they've made a mistake.

The phrase "if they've made a mistake" might lead you to use an `if` statement to deal with this situation. In other words, you might be led to think the solution is something like the following (in pseudocode):

```
Prompt the user to enter their age;
Read the user's response;
Assign the response to the variable named age;

if (age is negative) {
    Prompt the user to enter their age;
    Read the user's response;
```

```
    Assign the response to the variable named age;
}

Use the variable named age;
```

You would then test your program, see it works correctly, and deploy it. Unfortunately, at some point, the user will probably enter an invalid response to **both** prompts, and the program will fail (in one way or another).

Because beginning programmers tend to get locked into a particular solution, you might then "correct" the code as follows:

```
Prompt the user to enter their age;
Read the user's response;
Assign the response to the variable named age;

if (age is negative) {
    Prompt the user to enter their age;
    Read the user's response;
    Assign the response to the variable named age;

    if (age is negative) {
        Prompt the user to enter their age;
        Read the response;
        Assign the response to the variable named age;
    }
}

Use the variable named age;
```

Of course, this doesn't correct the defect at all. That is, this code will only work for two or fewer invalid responses, and there is no limit on the number of times that the user can enter an invalid response.

Review

What you need is a way to repeat a block of code an indefinite number of times (i.e., until the user enters a valid response). The phrase "repeat a block of code" should immediately bring to mind a loop of some kind. The phrase "an indefinite number of times" should bring to mind a `while` or `do` loop. In other words, you are already partway to a solution.

As you know, a `while` loop is appropriate if the body needn't be executed, and a `do` loop is appropriate if the body must be executed at least once. So, you might be thinking that the solution to the reprompting problem involves a `while` loop since you don't always need to reprompt. The truth is slightly more complicated than that.

Thinking About The Problem

It turns out that there are, in fact, two different versions of this problem. In the first, the initial prompt and the subsequent prompts (i.e., after the user provides an invalid response) are the same. In the second, the initial prompt is different from the subsequent prompts. What this means is that a `do` loop is appropriate in solutions of the first version, and a `while` loop is appropriate in solutions of the second version.

The Pattern

The pattern that solves the first version of this problem can be described as follows:

1. Enter a `do` loop. In the body of the loop:
    1.1. Prompt the user.
    1.2. Retrieve the user's response.
2. Repeat when the response is invalid.

The pattern that solves the second version of this problem can be described as follows:

1. Prompt the user with the normal message.
2. Retrieve the user's response.
3. Enter a `while` loop when the response is invalid. In the body of the loop:
    3.1. Prompt the user with the alternate message.
    3.2. Retrieve the response.
4. Repeat.

Examples

In the following examples, the user is prompted to enter an

age which must be non-negative to be valid. In the first version, the user is always provided with the same prompt:

```
do {
    System.out.printf("Enter a non-negative age: ");
    age = scanner.nextInt();
} while (age < 0);
```

In the second version, the user is only told that the age must be non-negative after an invalid response is provided:

```
System.out.printf("Enter your age: ");
age = scanner.nextInt();
while (age < 0) {
    System.out.printf("  Enter a non-negative value: ");
    age = scanner.nextInt();
}
```

Note that, in general, there are many ways in which the user could respond inappropriately, not just by entering a negative number. For example, the user could enter a non-number when a number was required, enter a number that is too large, or enter a non-integer when an integer was required. In all of these cases, the pattern remains the same, all that changes is the `boolean` expression in the loop (and, perhaps, the way the response is read).

[13]

Accumulators

In some situations, the iterations of a loop are independent of each other. However, in many situations a program needs to "keep track of" something over the course of multiple iterations. In situations like these, accumulators often come into play.

Motivation

If you ask someone "on the street" how to add a column of numbers by hand, they will probably say something like "just add them up". If you then ask them to demonstrate with a column of fifty **single-digit** numbers, they probably won't have any trouble. However, if you talk to them while they're doing it (especially if you drop some numbers into the conversation), they'll have much more difficulty, and may not be able to do it at all.

If you then suggest that they "write things down" as they go, there's a good chance that they won't know what you mean and/or how that would help. The reason is that, when adding single-digit numbers, people use their brain both to add pairs of numbers and to store the result, and they can't imagine how to use paper for storage. However, as you know, when writing a program you must carefully differentiate between the two.

Review

Suppose you need to write a program that operates on all of the elements of an array of numbers (e.g., `double` values). You will immediately recognize that you need to use a loop. Hopefully, because it's a *determinate* (or *definite*) loop (i.e., the number of iterations is known), you will also recognize that you should use a `for` loop.

For example, given an array named `data` that contains `n` elements, you might start with code like the following:

```
for (int i = 0; i < n; i++) {
    // Do something with data[i]
}
```

To go from here to a program that calculates the sum, you need to think about what needs to be done with each element of the array (i.e., each `data[i]` in the example) in order to calculate the sum.

Thinking About The Problem

Returning to the person on the street, suppose you again ask them to find the sum of fifty single-digit numbers and describe what they are doing while they are doing it. Suppose further that the numbers start with 7, 3, and 2. Most likely, they will say something like "7 plus 3 is 10, plus 2 is 12, ...". Which is to say, they will use what is commonly called a *running total*.

If you now point this out to them, they will probably be able to use a piece of paper to store the running total, rather than their brain. This is exactly the same technique that you need to use when writing a program for this purpose. That is, you need a variable, called an *accumulator*, to store the running total.

The Pattern

The accumulator pattern involves declaring a variable of appropriate type in which the running value can be stored, initializing this variable to an appropriate value, and then using the updating pattern from Chapter 1 to (potentially) change the value each iteration.

In the context of finding the sum of an array of `double` values, this pattern is realized as follows:

```
double total;
int n;

n = data.length;
total = 0.0;

for (int i = 0; i < n; i++) {
    total += data[i];
}
```

In this realization, `total` is declared to be a `double` because the sum of an array of `double` values is a `double`, it is initialized to `0` because the sum of an array containing no elements is zero, and at each iteration `total` is increased by the value of `data[i]`.

Examples

An accumulator can be of almost any type and can be used for a variety of different purposes. Several examples should make the flexibility of this pattern apparent.

Numeric Examples

In addition to finding the sum, numeric accumulators can be used for many other purposes. For example, you can use a numeric accumulator to find either the minimum or the maximum of an array of double values. This is illustrated for the maximum below:

```
double maximum;
int n;

n = data.length;
maximum = Double.NEGATIVE_INFINITY;

for (int i = 0; i < n; i++)
    if (data[i] > maximum) maximum = data[i];
}
```

The accumulator (now named `maximum`) is initialized to the lower bound on `double` values (which is defined in a static attribute of the `Double` class named `Double.NEGATIVE_INFINITY`), and it is only updated at iteration i if data[i] is greater than the running maximum that has been found so far.

Boolean Examples

Boolean accumulators are commonly used for containment checks (i.e., to determine if an array contains a particular target value). The following example determines if the double value named target equals any element of the double array named data:

```
boolean       found;
int           n;

n = data.length;
found = false;

for (int i = 0; ((i < n) && !found); i++) {
    if (target == data[i]) found = true;
}
```

The accumulator in this case is the boolean variable named found. It is important to note that this method does not assign false to found when target does not equal data[i], as this is the default value of found. Note also that, though it isn't necessary to do so, this method breaks out of the loop as soon as found is true. It other words, it only iterates as long as both i < n evaluates to true and !found evaluates to true.[1]

Examples with Multiple Accumulators

Sometimes it is convenient or even necessary to use two accumulators in the same loop. In the following example, one accumulator named total contains the running total, and another accumulator named lowest contains the running minimum:

```
double lowest, result, total;
int n;

n = data.length;
total = 0.0;
lowest = Double.POSITIVE_INFINITY;
```

1. If you know about the break statement, you could also use it in the body of the if statement to break out of the loop.

```
for (int i = 0; i < n; i++) {
    total += data[i];
    if (data[i] < lowest) lowest = data[i];
}
result = (total - lowest) / (n - 1);
```

It then returns the mean of the elements of the array after having dropped the minimum. While one could accomplish the same thing using two loops (one to calculate the running total and one to calculate the minimum), it is much more elegant to use one loop and two accumulators.[2]

As another example, suppose you want to find **not** the maximum of an array, but, instead, the index of the largest element (often called the *argmax*, the argument that maximizes the "function", as opposed to the *max*). One way to do this is to use one accumulator to keep track of the maximum and another to keep track of its index as follows:

```
double maximum;
int index, n;

n = data.length;
maximum = Double.NEGATIVE_INFINITY;
index = -1;

for (int i = 0; i < n; i++) {
    if (data[i] > maximum) {
        index   = i;
        maximum = data[i];
    }
}
```

A Warning

Some people like to initialize the accumulator to a "smarter" value. For example, when calculating the running total, some people like to initialize the accumulator to the 0th element of the array rather than 0 as follows:

```
double total;
int n;

n = data.length;
```

2. This implementation assumes that the array has at least 2 elements. A more robust implementation would ensure that this is the case.

```
// Initialize to element 0
total = data[0];

// Start with element 1
for (int i = 1; i < n; i++) {
    total += data[i];
}
```

The purported advantage of this approach is that there is one less iteration of the loop.

As another example, when calculating the maximum, some people like to initialize the accumulator to the 0th element of the array rather than `Double.NEGATIVE_INFINITY` as follows:

```
double maximum;
int n;

n = data.length;

// Initialize to element 0
maximum = data[0];

// Start with element 1
for (int i = 1; i < n; i++) {
    if (data[i] > maximum) maximum = data[i];
}
```

Again, this has the advantage of one fewer iterations. It also has the advantage of not having to treat `Double.NEGATIVE_INFINITY` as a special case.

The shortcoming of this approach is that arrays of length `0` must be treated as a special case. That is, if the array contains no elements, then initializing the accumulator to element `0` of the array will throw an exception (at run-time) when the array has no elements. Hence, one must **first** check to ensure that the array has a length of at least `1`.

In some circumstances, this may be worthwhile. For example, the argmax code can be written using just the accumulator named `index` by changing the initialization and the expression in the `if` statement as follows:

```
double maximum;
int index, n;

n = data.length;

// Initialize to element 0
index = 0;
```

```
// Start with element 1
for (int i = 1; i < n; i++) {
    if (data[i] > data[index]) index = i;
}
```

Whether this trade-off is worthwhile is a matter of personal preference.

Looking Ahead

Though you may not have used `String` objects other than for output yet, you will soon, and they can and are used as accumulators in a variety of different ways. They are commonly used with the concatenation operator, to combine `String` objects into a longer `String`.

For example, the following code uses an array of `String` objects containing the parts of a person's name (e.g., personal name, "middle" name, and family name) and constructs a Gmail address from them:

```
int n;
String address;

n = name.length;
if (n == 0) {
    address = "no-reply";
} else {
    address = name[0];
    for (int i = 1; i < n; i++) {
        address += "." + name[i];
    }
}
address += "@gmail.com";
```

The accumulator in this case (named `address`) creates a long `String` that contains all the parts of the person's name, with periods between them.

[14]

Accumulator Arrays

Programs often need to keep track of (in one way or another) multiple things over multiple iterations. In some cases, this can be accomplished with multiple accumulators of the kind discussed in Chapter 13. However, in other cases, it is better to use an array of accumulators.

Motivation

Many K-12 schools assign numeric grades (on a scale of 0 to 100) to individual students during the year and then, at the end of the year, create a summary report that shows the number of students that were in each centile (i.e., the 90s, the 80s, etc.). If you were asked to write a program for this purpose, you'd know (from Chapter 13) that you should use an accumulator to keep a running count of the number of students in each centile. Since there are eleven different centiles (treating 100 as an entire centile), this means that you need eleven different accumulators.

Review

If you approached the problem in this way, you might proceed by declaring and initializing eleven different accumulators as follows:

```
int ones, tens, twentys, thirtys, fortys, fiftys, sixtys,
```

```
    seventys, eightys, ninetys, hundreds;

ones = tens = twentys = thirtys = fortys = fiftys
    = sixtys = seventys = eightys = ninetys = hundreds = 0;
```

You then might write the following loop to update these accumulators:

```
int n = data.length;

for (int i = 0; i < n; i++) {
    if      (data[i] <  10) ones++;
    else if (data[i] <  20) tens++;
    else if (data[i] <  30) twentys++;
    else if (data[i] <  40) thirtys++;
    else if (data[i] <  50) fortys++;
    else if (data[i] <  60) fiftys++;
    else if (data[i] <  70) sixtys++;
    else if (data[i] <  80) seventys++;
    else if (data[i] <  90) eightys++;
    else if (data[i] < 100) ninetys++;
    else                    hundreds++;
}
```

Unfortunately, there are three big shortcomings of this approach. First, all of the variables must be declared and initialized individually, and, while its only mildly awkward in this case, if you needed more accumulators it would become very awkward. Second, the nested `if` statement that is used to update the appropriate accumulator is both awkward, tedious, and error-prone. Finally, since methods in Java can only return a single entity, you could not write a re-usable method to return all of the calculated values, you would have to copy it to wherever it was needed.

As you should know, in situations like this (i.e., when you have multiple "related" values) it is better to use an array than to use individual variables. What you may not yet know is how to use an array to solve the centile histogram problem.

Thinking About The Problem

The first thing to realize is that the variables `ones`, `tens`, etc. can be replaced with an array named `count`. Specifically, `count[0]` will replace `ones`, `count[1]` will replace `tens`, etc.[1] This facilitates both the declaration and the initialization.

The second thing to realize is that the truncation pattern from Chapter 5 can be used to calculate the index associated with a particular centile. Specifically, one can truncate to the 10s place to get the centile. For example, a value of `63` is in centile `63/10` (i.e., centile 6; the 60s), a value of `8` is in centile `8/10` (i.e., centile 0; the 1s), and a value of `100` is in centile `100/10` (i.e., centile 10; the 100s). This eliminates the need for a complicated `if` statement.

The Pattern

The pattern, then, can be stated as follows:

1. Declare and initialize an array to hold the number of accumulators needed.
2. Create an algorithm for identifying the index of the particular accumulator that needs to be updated during a particular iteration.
3. Write a loop that calculates the index and updates the appropriate accumulator.

In most situations, this logic should be encapsulated in a method.

Examples

A few examples should help you see how you can use this pattern in a wide variety of situations.

The Motivating Example

Continuing with the grading example, this pattern can be implemented as follows:

1. Note that centiles involve the powers of 10. So, you should not be surprised to see a similarity between the way the centiles are counted and the way the digits in a decimal (i.e., base 10) number were counted in Chapters 3 and Chapter 11.

```
public static int[] gradeHistogram(int[] data) {
    int   centile, n;
    int[] count = {0, 0, 0, 0, 0, 0, 0, 0, 0, 0, 0};

    n = data.length;

    for (int i = 0; i < n; i++) {
        centile = data[i] / 10;
        count[centile] += 1;
    }

    return count;
}
```

The expression `data[i] / 10` is used to calculate the index (i.e., the centile) of `data[i]` in the accumulator array, and the statement `count[centile] += 1;` increases the value of the $\texttt{centile}^{th}$ accumulator by `1`.

Some Other Examples

This pattern works best when the algorithm for calculating the index of the accumulator is straightforward. For example, suppose you need to count the number of odd and even values in an array. If the number of even values is stored in element `0` and the number of odd elements is stored in element `1`, then you can implement this pattern as follows:

```
public static int[] oddsAndEvens(int[] data) {
    int[] count = {0, 0};
    int n = data.length;

    for (int i = 0; i < n; i++) {
        count[data[i] % 2] += 1;
    }

    return count;
}
```

This works because, as you know from Chapter 4, `data[i]` is even when `(data[i] % 2)` is `0` and is odd when `(data[i] % 2)` is `1`.

However, in some cases you can't (or it is awkward to) avoid the use of a complicated `if` statement. For example, suppose you need to count the number of negative, zero, and positive elements in an array. You can implements this as follows:

```
public static int[] signs(int[] data) {
```

```
        int[] count = {0, 0, 0};
        int n = Array.getLength(data);

        for (int i = 0; i < n; i++) {
            if      (data[i] <  0) count[0]++;
            else if (data[i] == 0) count[1]++;
            else                   count[2]++;
        }
        return count;
    }
```

Notice that, even though this implementation uses a nested `if` statement, there are benefits to using an accumulator array. First, it facilitates the declaration and initialization of the accumulators. Second, all of the accumulators can be returned by returning the array.

[15]

Lookup Arrays

Even beginning programmers quickly realize that arrays make it very easy to perform the same operation(s) on each element of a homogeneous group of elements. However, what they often don't realize is that arrays can be used in less obvious ways as well. Lookup arrays are one example.

Motivation

Highway exits used to be numbered using consecutive integers. The first (on a particular highway) was exit 1, the second was exit 2, etc. Later, highway exit numbers were changed to correspond (at least closely) to the mile marker (i.e., the number of miles since the start of the highway). So, the exit at mile marker 1 is numbered 1, the exit at mile marker 15 is numbered 15, etc. The problem then arises of how to "convert" an old exit number to a new exit number.

Review

As you know, arrays have two important characteristics. First, each element must be of the same type (i.e., the elements must be *homogeneous*). Second, the indexes are consecutive, non-negative `int` values. However, beyond that, there are no restrictions on how they can be used.

When you are first introduced to arrays, the examples all tend to involve "data processing" of some kind. For example, they involve weekly sales, annual populations, grades on exams, etc., and the indexes are just used to differentiate the elements. However, the values of the indexes can be meaningful in their own right. For example, in the current context, the indexes could represent exit numbers.

Thinking About The Problem

All that remains to think about is whether the indexes should represent the old exit numbers or the new exit numbers. Fortunately, given the nature of the old and new exit numbers, the correct representational scheme is obvious. Except for the fact that array indexes start at 0, they seem to have the same properties as the old highway numbering system. So, if there are five exits, you can use an array of length six (with indexes of `0`, `1`, ..., `5`) to hold information about each exit. In this case, the information that you want to associate with each old exit number is the new exit number, which is, itself, an `int`. So, you can keep the information you need in an `int[]` of length six.

For example, if the new exit numbers are at mile markers 1, 15, 16, 28, and 35, you can store them in the following `static` array named `NEW_NUMBERS`:

```
private static final int[] NEW_NUMBERS = {-1, 1, 15, 16, 28, 35};
```

where the first element is `-1` to indicate that there is no old exit number 0. This is illustrated in Figure 15.1.

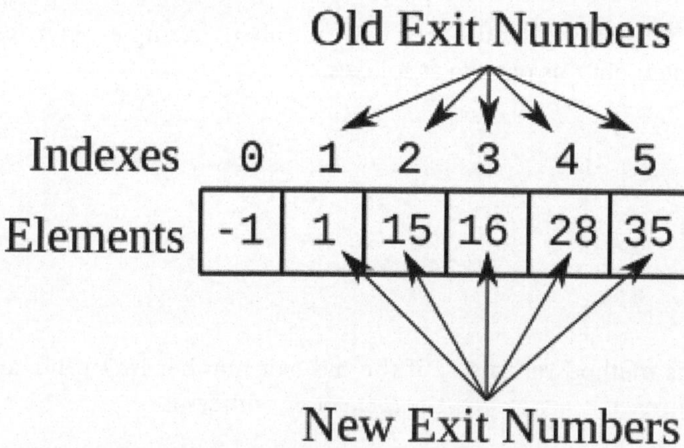

Figure 15.1. The Correspondence between Old and New Exit Numbers

Then, the new exit number corresponding to old exit number `i` is just `NEW_NUMBERS[i]`. For example, `NEW_NUMBERS[3]` is the new exit number that corresponds to old exit number `3`.

The Pattern

The pattern follows immediately from this example:

1. Create an array in which the indexes correspond to the *key* that will be used to perform the look-up, and the elements correspond to the *value* that is to be determined.
2. Create a method that validates the key and returns the appropriate element of the array for any valid key (and an error status for any invalid key).

Examples

Some other examples will help illustrate both the power and limitations of this pattern.

The Motivating Example

Continuing with the exit number example, you can implement this pattern as follows:

```
private static final int[] NEW_NUMBERS = {-1, 1, 15, 16, 28, 35};

public static int newExitNumberFor(int oldExitNumber) {
    if ((oldExitNumber > 5)) {
        return -1;
    } else {
        return NEW_NUMBERS[oldExitNumber];
    }
}
```

This method returns `-1` if the old exit number isn't valid, and returns `NEW_NUMBERS[oldExitNumber]` otherwise.

Non-Integer Values

Of course, though the indexes must be integers (because of the nature of arrays)[1], the values needn't be. This is easy to illustrate in an example that looks up the name of the exit that corresponds to an old exit number:

```
private static final String[] NAMES = {"", "Willow Ave.",
    "Broad St.", "Downtown", "North End", "Lake Dr."};

public static String exitNameFor(int oldExitNumber) {
    if ((oldExitNumber > 5)) {
        return "";
    } else {
        return NAMES[oldExitNumber];
    }
}
```

"Large" Contiguous Keys

The previous examples have keys that are contiguous and start at 0 or 1, like the indexes of an array. As a result, they are particularly well-suited to this pattern. However, it should be immediately obvious that the keys don't have to start at 0 or 1. For example, you could use the year as a key to lookup annual data of some kind. You then need only subtract the given key from the "base" year in order to get the index.

1. Chapter 17 on conformal arrays discusses one way to circumvent this limitation.

For example, suppose you need to look up the annual sales revenues (in hundreds of thousands of dollars) for a company that was established in 2015. You need only subtract `2015` from the key in order to get the index, as follows:

```
private static final double[] SALES = {
    107.2, 225.1, 189.9, 263.2};

public static double sales(int year) {
    if ((year >= 2019)) {
        return 0.0; // No sales
    } else {
        int index;
        index = year - 2015;
        return SALES[index];
    }
}
```

Non-Contiguous Keys

Though the keys in the previous examples are contiguous, the pattern can often be used with non-contiguous but regular keys by employing the digit manipulation pattern from Chapter 3, the arithmetic on the circle pattern from Chapter 4, or the truncation pattern from Chapter 5. For example, suppose you want to be able to look-up the letter grade (either A, B, C, D, or F) for a particular numeric grade (an `int` in the interval $[0, 100]$). You could implement this as follows:

```
private static final char[] GRADES = {
    'F', 'F', 'F', 'F', 'F', 'F', 'D', 'C', 'B', 'A', 'A'};

public static char letterGrade(int numberGrade) {
    int index;

    index = numberGrade / 10;
    return GRADES[index];
}
```

In this example, a grade in the 90s or 100 corresponds to an A, a grade in the 80s corresponds to a B, etc. Then, to calculate the index from the key you need only divide by 10.

If, instead, one wanted to convert from a numeric grade to either "Pass" or "Fail", one could do the following:

```
private static final char[] STATUS = {'F', 'P'};
```

public static char passFail(double grade) { int index; index = (int) (grade / 60.0); return STATUS[index]; }

Finally, suppose you wanted to look-up the U.S. population for a particular census year. You could do the following:

```
private static final double[] POP = {
    3.9, 5.2, 7.2, 9.6, 12.9, 17.1, 23.1, 31.4, 38.6, 49.4, 63.0, 76.2,
    92.2, 106.0, 123.2, 132.2, 151.3, 179.3, 203.2, 226.5, 248.7, 281.4,
    308.7};

public static double population(int year) {
    int index;

    if ((year >= 2020)) {
        return 1.0;
    } else {
        index = (year - 1790) / 10;
        return POP[index];
    }
}
```

To get the index from the key in this case, you first subtract the base year (i.e., 1790, the year of the first census) from the key and then divide the result by 10 (because the census has been conducted every 10 years since the base year) to get the index.

Keys with Multiple Parts

It should be clear that, if you want to use months as the key, then you should use a 0-based index (i.e., in which `0` denotes January, `1` denotes February, etc.). It should also be clear that, if you want to use (contiguous) years as keys, then you should subtract the base year from the year of interest. Suppose, however, that you have monthly values that span multiple years. In this case, the key has multiple parts (i.e., the month and year of interest).

Fortunately, it is easy to combine several ideas to find the index of interest. In particular, you can use an expression like the following:

```
index = (year - BASE_YEAR) + month;
```

where the purpose of the different variables/constants should be obvious.

Looking Ahead

The process of turning a key of any kind into an integer (in a particular range) is known as *hashing*. It is one of the most important topics covered in courses on data structures and algorithms. This chapter has used some very simple and intuitive hash functions, but hash functions can be quite sophisticated, and understanding their properties can require serious thought.

[16]

Interval Membership

There are many situations in which categories are defined by intervals and, as a result, it is necessary to find the interval that contains a particular value. This chapter considers one specific way to organize the data and perform such a search.

Motivation

The U.S. tax code defines a group of intervals called *tax brackets*, each of which has an associated *marginal tax rate*. In 2017, these tax brackets (for single taxpayers) were defined as in Table 16.1. For example, a person earning $23,000 would be in the 15% marginal bracket (i.e., would pay 10.0% on the first $9,325, and 15.0% on everything over $9,325).

Our objective in this chapter is to organize the information in Table 16.1 in such a way that it is easy to find the marginal tax rate for any income.

Table 16.1. U.S. Tax Brackets for Single Taxpayers in 2017

From	To	Rate
0	9,325	10.0
9,326	37,950	15.0
37,951	91,900	25.0
91,901	191,650	28.0
191,651	416,700	33.0
416,701	418,400	35.0
418,401	Above	39.6

Review

Though Chapter 15 on lookup arrays used different terminology, some of the examples were closely related to the problem considered here. For example, consider the problem of finding the letter grade that corresponds to a particular numerical grade. Essentially, one needs to find the interval that contains the numerical grade. However, since all of the intervals are the same size, there is no reason to explicitly list the intervals. Hence, the code in Chapter 15 converts an interval like $[90, 99]$ to the index 9. In this chapter, the situations involve intervals which are *irregular*, and a different solution is required.

Thinking About The Problem

The tax table has two convenient properties (that are common to a wide variety of similar situations). First, the union of all of the intervals is the relevant subset of the real numbers (in this case, the non-negative reals). In other words, the tax table contains the marginal tax rate for every possible income. Second, the intervals are *disjoint*. That is, the intersection of any two intervals is the empty set.

Hence, each income has a unique marginal tax rate that can be determined using only a sequence of boundary values, $b_0, b_1, \ldots, b_{n-1}$. Specifically, assuming you want to "cover" the entire set of real numbers, interval 0 can be defined as

$[-\infty, b_0)$, interval 1 can be defined as $[b_0, b_1)$, interval 2 can be defined as $[b_1, b_2)$, interval $n-1$ can be defined as $[b_{n-2}, b_{n-1})$, and interval n can be defined as $[b_{n-1}, \infty)$. For the tax example, the boundaries for single taxpayers are 0, 9326, 37951, 91901, 191651, 416701, 418401, making the intervals $[-\infty, 0)$, $[0, 9326)$, $[9326, 37951)$, $[37951, 91901)$, $[91901, 191651)$, $[191651, 416701)$, $[416701, 418401)$, $[418401, \infty)$.

Since the boundaries are homogeneous (i.e., they are values of the same type) they can be stored in a single array. For example, the boundaries for single taxpayers can be stored in a `int[]` named `single` as follows:

```
int[] single  = {0, 9326, 37951, 91901, 191651, 416701, 418401};
```

Given this representation of the intervals, you could search through them as follows:

```
public static int indexOf(int value, int[] boundary) {
    int        i, n;

    n = boundary.length;

    for (i = 0; i < n-1; ++i) {
        if ((value >= boundary[i]) && (value < boundary[i + 1])) {
            return i + 1;
        }
    }

    return n;
}
```

The Pattern

While the implementation above is fine, it has a couple of shortcomings. First, it uses a `for` loop, which might lead someone reading the code to think that the loop is determinate (or definite) when, in fact, it isn't. That is, someone reading the code might assume that there are always exactly `n-1` iterations when there can be fewer. Second, the containment condition checks to see if the target value is greater than or equal to the left boundary and less then the right boundary at every iteration. However, both checks aren't really necessary since the right boundary of interval $n - 1$ is the same as the left boundary of interval n.

The first shortcoming can be corrected by using a `while` loop. The second shortcoming can be corrected by continuing to loop as long as the target value is greater than or equal to the right boundary (meaning that the correct interval has not yet been found). Combining the two ideas leads to the following pattern:

```
public static int indexOf(int value, int[] boundary) {
    int      i, n;

    n = boundary.length;

    i = 0;
    while ((i < n) && (value >= boundary[i]))  ++i;

    return i;
}
```

This algorithm increases the index as long as there are more intervals to check and the target value is greater than or equal to the right boundary.

Examples

Continuing with the tax example, you can now find the tax bracket for a particular income level as follows:

```
int[] single = {0, 9326, 37951, 91901, 191651, 416701, 418401};

int bracket;
bracket = indexOf(125350, single);
```

You can then use a lookup-array (see Chapter 15) to find the marginal tax rate that corresponds to that tax bracket as follows:

```
double[] rate = {-1.0, 10.0, 15.0, 25.0, 28.0, 33.0, 35.0, 39.6};

double marginal;
marginal = rate[bracket];
```

Some Warnings

The obvious thing to be careful about when using this

pattern is which side of the interval is open and which side is closed. Making mistakes here can cause *off-by-one defects* that are difficult to find.

The other thing to be careful about is much less obvious. One might be tempted to combine the interval membership functionality and the look-up array functionality in a single method. For example, in the tax rate example, one might be tempted to do the following:

```
public static double taxRate(int income) {
    int[] single  = {0, 9326, 37951, 91901, 191651, 416701, 418401};
    double[] rate = {-1.0, 10.0, 15.0, 25.0, 28.0, 33.0, 35.0, 39.6};

    return rate[indexOf(income, single)];
}
```

The drawback of this seemingly elegant idea is that one often wants to perform more than one lookup with the same index.

Perhaps the easiest way to see this is with the grade example from Chapter 15 on lookup arrays. One commonly wants to convert a numeric grade on a 0–100 scale to **both** a letter grade on an F–A scale and a numeric grade on a 0–4 scale. Hence, one wants to do one interval membership search and two array look-ups. This can be accomplished as follows:

```
int[] intervals = {0, 60, 63, 67, 70, 73, 77, 80, 83, 87, 90, 93};

double[] gp = { -1.0, 0.0, 0.7, 1.0, 1.3, 1.7, 2.0, 2.3, 2.7, 3.0, 3.3, 3.7, 4.0};

String[] letter = { "NA","F","D-","D","D+","C-","C","C+","B-","B","B+","A-","A"};

int i;
String out;
i = indexOf(88, intervals); o
ut = String.format("Grade: %s (%3.1f)", letter[i], gp[i]);
```

There's no reason to do the interval membership search separately for each of the two look-ups. Hence, it is better to have a separate `indexOf()` method.

Looking Ahead

In some situations, the intervals don't cover all the real numbers (i.e., there are gaps). In such situations, the value might not be in any interval. One way to handle this (and other situations) is to use *conformal arrays* as discussed in Chapter 17 —

use one array to hold the left boundaries and another to hold the right boundaries.

[17]

Conformal Arrays

In many situations there are multiple pieces of data that need to be organized in a way that makes them easy to work with. While this problem can sometimes be solved with a single array, many other times a more powerful organizational scheme is needed. This is where conformal arrays come in.

Motivation

The Federal Reserve Bank tracks monthly data about many aspects of the economy. Suppose you are working with a group that has developed a categorical measure of consumer confidence. The group wants to explore the relationships between its measure of consumer confidence, the consumer price index (CPI), the civilian unemployment rate (in percent), and the M2 money stock (in billions of dollars) for the year 2018 (on a monthly basis). You need to organize this information in such a way that it can be used to conduct a variety of different analyses.

Review

As you know, arrays make it very easy to perform the same operation(s) on homogeneous values. So, if you were only interested in the CPI, for example, you could store it in a `double[]` with twelve elements (since there are twelve months in the year 2018). Such an array is referred to as a *time series* because the index is a measure of time.

However, you need to organize more than just the CPI. You need to organize all 48 data points (12 months of data for 4 different time series) and 12 associated labels (the three-letter abbreviations for the months). Since the elements aren't homogeneous (i.e., some are numbers and some are three-letter abbreviations), you can't use a single array.

Thinking About The Problem

Conceptually, the data in this example can be thought of as a table. In fact, time series data (like the data in this example) are often presented in tabular form, as illustrated in Table 17.1. In this case, the table has one column for each type of data and one row for each month.

Table 17.1. U.S. Macroeconomic Data for 2018 (Not Seasonally Adjusted)

Month	CPI	Unemployment	M2	Confidence
Jan	247.867	4.5	13855.1	Low
Feb	248.991	4.4	13841.2	Low
Mar	249.554	4.1	14022.9	Moderate
Apr	250.546	3.7	14064.4	High
May	251.588	3.6	13984.6	High
Jun	251.989	4.2	14079.2	Moderate
Jul	252.006	4.1	14113.8	Low
Aug	252.146	3.9	14170.3	Moderate
Sep	252.439	3.6	14204.7	Moderate
Oct	252.885	3.5	14211.6	High
Nov	252.038	3.5	14272.8	High
Dec	251.233	3.7	14473.0	High

While there are a variety of different ways of organizing tabular data, none of them are available to you at the moment. Fortunately, you can use multiple different arrays. Doing so just requires a little thought.

A table can be conceptualized in two ways. On the one hand, you can think about a table as consisting of rows, each of which consists of columns. The is called *row-major* form (i.e., rows first). On the other hand, you can think think about a table as consisting of columns, each of which consists of rows. This is called *column-major* form. In the first case, one array can be used to store each row; in the second case, one array can be used to store each column

Regardless of which approach you use, the arrays will be conformal. That is, they will share a common index. If you use one array for each column then the common index will be the conceptual row headers. In the example above, if you use this approach, the indexes will correspond to the months. On the other hand, if you use one array for each row then the common index will be the column headers. In the example above, if you use this approach, the indexes will correspond to “Month”, “CPI”, “Unemployment”, “M2”, and “Confidence”.

The Pattern

To obtain a solution to the problem you need only decide whether to use an array for each column or an array for each row. Fortunately, in most situations, this is an easy decision to make. Specifically, you should choose the alternative that satisfies the following criteria:

1. The elements of the array must be of the same type; and
2. The indexes must be easily representable as `int` values.

In many situations, only one alternative will satisfy both criteria.

Each such conformal array can then be thought of as an individual *field* in a *record* that has an index number. So, if you have two arrays named `fieldA` and `fieldB`, then record number `i` consists of `fieldA[i]` and `fieldB[i]`. This is illustrated in Figure 17.1 for some data about four different people. The names of the people are stored in the `String[]` named `fieldA`, and the number of science fiction books they own are stored in the `int[]` named `fieldB`.

```
String[] fieldA = {"Alice", "Bob", "Carol", "Dinesh"};
int[]    fieldB = {    105,    98,     317,      148};
```

Record 2

Figure 17.1. An Illustration of Conformal Arrays

Examples

Continuing with the economic example above, its useful to consider both possible approaches for the tabular representation in Table 17.1.

If you were to use one array for each row then the first and last elements would need to be `String` objects and the middle three elements would need to be `double` values. Hence, this approach doesn't satisfy the first criterion and can be eliminated.

If you were to use one array for each column, then all of the elements of the first and last columns would be `String` objects and all of the elements of the three middle columns would be `double` values. Hence, the first criterion is satisfied. In addition, the second criterion is satisfied because you can use a 0-based `int` representation of the months (i.e., `0` for January, `1` for February, etc.).

This leads to the following conformal arrays:

```
// Month of the year
String[] month = {
    "Jan", "Feb", "Mar", "Apr", "May", "Jun",
    "Jul", "Aug", "Sep", "Oct", "Nov", "Dec" };

// Consumer price index for all urban consumers
// (not seasonally adjusted)
double[] cpiaucns = {
  247.867, 248.991, 249.554, 250.546, 251.588, 251.989,
  252.006, 252.146, 252.439, 252.885, 252.038, 251.233 };

// Unemployment rate (not seasonally adjusted)
double[] unratensa = {
    4.5, 4.4, 4.1, 3.7, 3.6, 4.2,
    4.1, 3.9, 3.6, 3.5, 3.5, 3.7 };
```

```
// M2 money stock (not seasonally adjusted)
double[] m2ns = {
    13855.1, 13841.2, 14022.9, 14064.4, 13984.6, 14079.2,
    14113.8, 14170.3, 14204.7, 14211.6, 14272.8, 14473.0 };

// Consumer confidence
String[] confidence = {
    "Low", "Low",        "Moderate", "High", "High", "Moderate",
    "Low", "Moderate", "Moderate", "High", "High", "High" };
```

Then, if you want to work with the CPI and M2 for May (month `4` in a 0-based numbering scheme), you simply need to use `cpiaucns[4]` and `m2ns[4]`. The corresponding abbreviation would then be `month[4]` and the corresponding consumer confidence would be `confidence[4]`.

A Warning

You might be tempted to use conformal arrays for solving the interval membership problem discussed in Chapter 16. That is, you might be tempted to create two arrays, `left` and `right`, that contain the left and right bounds for each interval. The shortcoming of this approach is that it is error-prone. In particular, observe that there is a very important constraint that involves `right[i]` and `left[i+1]` for element `i` (e.g., the two must be equal or differ by one, depending on exactly how they are used), and it is easy to inadvertently violate this constraint. Hence, unless there are gaps in the intervals, it is better to use a single array as described in Chapter 16.

Looking Ahead

It is often necessary to look-up information using a non-numeric key. How to do this efficiently is a topic for a course on data structures and algorithms. However, ignoring efficiency, conformal arrays are part of the answer.

To see how, consider the example above. Though it isn't necessary to do so, because you know how the months correspond to indexes in the other arrays, you could use the `month` array to find the index that corresponds to a particular month. In particular, consider the following method:

```
public static int find(String needle, String[] haystack) {
```

```
    int i, n;

    i = 0;
    n = haystack.length;
    while (i < n) {
        if (needle.equals(haystack[i])) {
            return i;
        }
        ++i;
    }
    return -1;
}
```

It returns the index of the element in `haystack` that equals the `needle`. You could then use this method to get the CPI and M2 for May as follows:

```
int i;
i = find("May", month);

// Do something with cpiaucns[i] and m2ns[i]
```

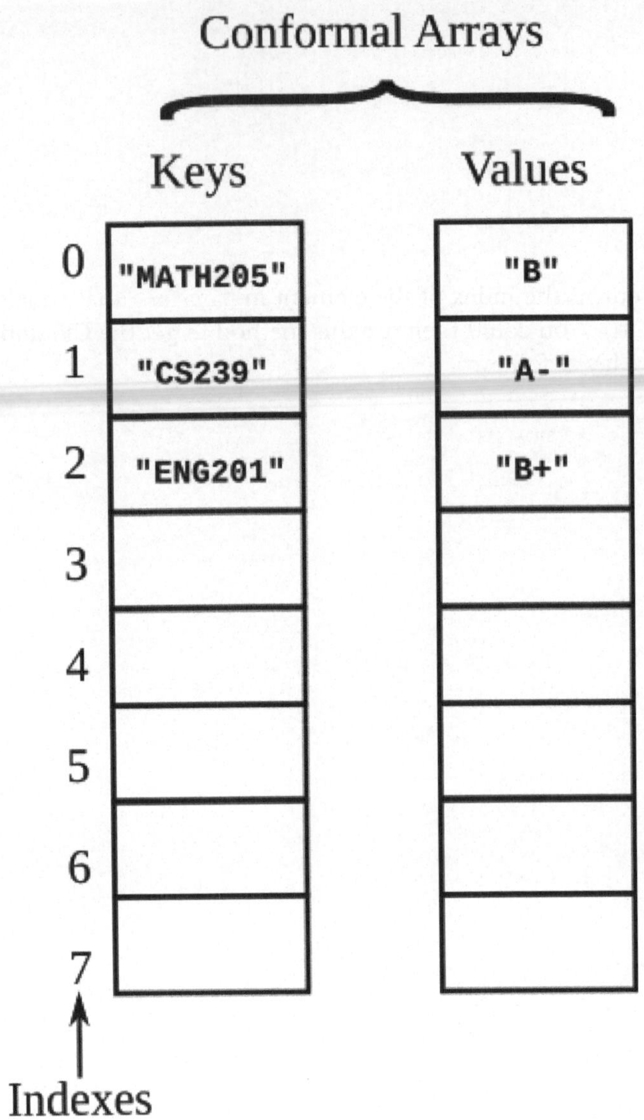

Figure 17.2. An Example of Keys and Values in Conformal Arrays

As another (more relevant) example, suppose you have conformal arrays that are holding course identifiers and the corresponding grades in those courses as in Figure 17.2. You could get the grade for a particular course using the following method:

```
public static String getGrade(String key,
                              String[] courses, String[] grades) {
    int     i, n;

    n = courses.length;
    i = 0;
    while (i < n) {
        if (key.equals(courses[i])) {
            return grades[i];
        }
        ++i;
    }
    return "NA";
}
```

[18]

Segmented Arrays

Recall that Chapter 17, on conformal arrays, discusses how multiple arrays can be used to organize records containing different fields (or tables containing rows and columns). This chapter considers a special case of this problem in which all of the elements of the records and fields (or rows and columns) are of the same type.

Motivation

Suppose you are working for a medical researcher who has collected data on the heights and weights of a variety of different people. You know from Chapter 17 that you could use two conformal arrays for this purpose, one containing the heights and one containing the weights (with the index used to identify the individual). However, since all of the measurements are `double` values, it's also possible to organize them in one array. Such an array is said to be *segmented* (or *packed*).

Review

Suppose you have two arrays of the same size, both of which contain `double` values. One array with twice as many elements could, obviously, hold all of the values in the two arrays. For example, suppose you have the following two arrays (each of length 4):

```
double[] heights = { 60.0,  62.0,  65.0,  70.0};
double[] weights = {100.0, 110.0, 120.0, 140.0};
```

Then, you could store all of the elements of both arrays in one array of length 8.

If you could then create an algorithm for finding/calculating the appropriate index, you could use this single array instead of the two individual arrays. Of course, the algorithm for finding/calculating the appropriate index is intimately related to the way in which the single array is organized. So, the two issues must be considered together.

Thinking About The Problem

While there are many ways of putting the elements from two arrays into one array (with twice the size), there are two that are particularly sensible. Each deserves some consideration.

In the first, you would *concatenate* the two arrays. That is, you would put the elements of one after the elements of the other.[1] This could be accomplished as follows:

```
int n = 4;
for (int i = 0; i < n; ++i) {
    concatenated[i]     = height[i];
}

for (int i = 0; i < n; ++i) {
    concatenated[n + i] = weight[i];
}
```

The first loop assigns element `i` of `height` to element `i` of `concatenated`, and the second loop assigns element `i` of `weight` to element `n+i` of `concatenated`. In other words, the first loop assigns the four elements of `height` to the first four elements of `concatenated`, and the second loop assigns the four elements of `weight` to the last four elements of `concatenated`.

Index:	0	1	2	3	4	5	6	7
	60.0	62.0	65.0	70.0	100.0	110.0	120.0	140.0

1. Which comes first doesn't matter, as long as you are consistent.

Figure 18.1. The Result of Concatenating two Arrays

Though it's not central to the point of this chapter, it should be clear to you that this same algorithm could be implemented with a single loop as follows:

```
int n = 4;
for (int i = 0; i < n; ++i) {
    concatenated[i]     = height[i];
    concatenated[n + i] = weight[i];
}
```

Regardless of the implementation, the end result is an array that is organized as in Figure 18.1.

In the second, you would interleave the two arrays. That is, you would alternate elements from the two arrays.[2] This could be accomplished as follows:

```
int n = 4;
for (int i = 0; i < n; ++i) {
    interleaved[2 * i]     = height[i];
    interleaved[2 * i + 1] = weight[i];
}
```

The first statement in the loop assigns elements 0, 1, 2, and 3 (i.e., the values of `i`) of `height` to elements 0, 2, 4, and 6 (i.e., the values of `2*i`) of `interleaved`. The second statement in the loop assigns elements 0, 1, 2, and 3 (i.e., the values of `i`) of `weight` to elements 1, 3, 5, and 7 (i.e., the values of `2*i+1`) of `interleaved`. The end result is an array that is organized as in Figure 18.2.

Index:	0	1	2	3	4	5	6	7
	60.0	100.0	62.0	110.0	65.0	120.0	70.0	140.0

Figure 18.2. The Result of Interleaving two Arrays

While both of these approaches work, the interleaved approach is more appropriate for the problem at hand. To see

2. Again, which comes first doesn't matter, as long as you are consistent.

why, consider Figure 18.3, which contains a more abstract conceptualization of the array in Figure 18.2. When interleaved, the fields of each record are kept together, making it easier to visualize the segmented array.

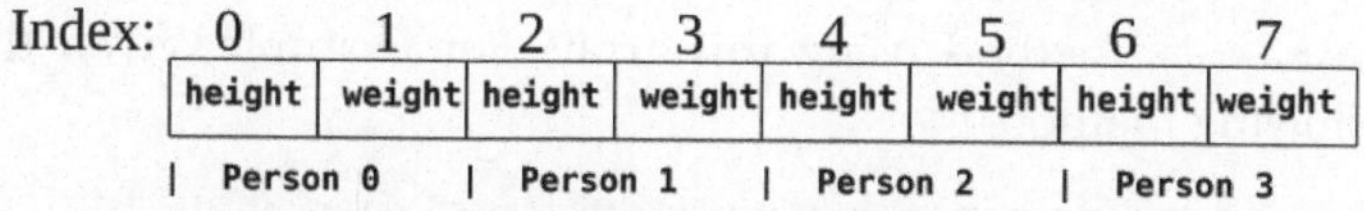

Figure 18.3. Conceptualizing the Interleaved Array of Weights and Heights

The Pattern

In general, if you let `recordSize` denote the number of fields in each record, `record` denote the record of interest (0-based), `field` denote the field of interest (also 0-based), and `index` denote the index of the element in the segmented array, then you can easily convert back and forth between the two approaches.

First, given the `record` and `field`, you can calculate the `index` as follows:

```
index = (record * recordSize) + field;
```

This is the same algorithm used in the loop to interleave the elements.

Second, given the `index`, you can calculate the `record` and `field` as follows:

```
record = index / recordSize;
field  = index % recordSize;
```

Note that this algorithm uses the techniques for arithmetic on the circle from Chapter 4.

Examples

Segmented arrays are most frequently used with `String` objects because they can be used to represent many other data types. One very common use involves command-line arguments.

Recall that the main() method of a Java application has a single String[] parameter, commonly named args. When an application is executed from the command line, all of the String objects after the name of the main class are passed to the main() method using this array. For example, given the following method:

```
public static int toIndex(int record, int field, int recordSize) {
    return (record * recordSize) + field;
}
```

you could pass the heights and weights of multiple people into main() as an interleaved array of String objects named args and "extract" information as needed. For example, if you wanted to assign the weight and height of person 1 to the variables w and h, respectively, you could do so as follows:

```
    h = Double.parseDouble(args[toIndex(1, 0, 2)]);
    w = Double.parseDouble(args[toIndex(1, 1, 2)]);
```

toIndex(1, 0, 2) evaluates to 2, so element 2 of args (i.e., "62.0" using the data from Figure 18.2) would be passed to Double.parseDouble(), and 62.0 would be assigned to h. Similarly, toIndex(1, 1, 2) evaluates to 3, so element 3 of args (i.e., "110.0" using the data from Figure 18.2) would be passed to Double.parseDouble(), and 110.0 would be assigned to w.

You could, of course, include the same logic in a loop and extract all of the heights and weights in the command-line arguments into conformal arrays as follows:

```
int recordSize = 2;
int records = args.length / recordSize;

for (int r = 0; r < records; ++r) {
    height[r] = Double.parseDouble(args[toIndex(r, 0, recordSize)]);
    weight[r] = Double.parseDouble(args[toIndex(r, 1, recordSize)]);
}
```

You could then work with the conformal arrays height and weight as you did in Chapter 17.

Looking Ahead

If you take a course on systems programming you will probably work with packed integers, a pattern that is related to segmented/packed arrays. The difference is that, rather than working with the elements of an array, you will work with portions of the integer (as, for example, was briefly discussed at the end of Chapter 3 on digit manipulation and in Chapter 10 on bit flags).

For example, because of the way the eye processes light, many visual output devices represent colors using a red component, a green component, and a blue component, each of which can take on 256 different possible values. Since each component can be represented in 8 bits, it is possible to represent a color using a single 32-bit `int` (with 8 bits to spare).

Suppose you want to ignore the highest-order (i.e., left-most) 8 bits, use the next 8 bits for the red component, the next 8 bits for the green component, and the lowest-order (i.e., right-most) 8 bits for the blue component. Suppose, further, that you want to create an `int` that contains the following shade of purple:

```
int bb, gg, rr;
rr =  69;
gg =   0;
bb = 132;
```

In order to create the packed 32-bit integer, you need to shift the bits in the red component to the left by 16, the bits in the green component to the left by 8, and leave the bits in the blue component where they are (i.e., in the least-significant bits). Then, you need to combine them into a single `int` using bitwise "inclusive or" operators}. This can be accomplished as follows:

```
int color;
color = 0;
color |= (rr << 16) | (gg << 8) | (bb << 0);
```

This `int` will, of course, have a value (4522116 in this case), but it is of no interest. What's important, is that this `int` has several distinct components.

To extract the red, green, and blue components from the packed `int` you must invert the process. That is, you need to do a bitwise "and" with an appropriate mask, and then shift the bits to the right (to move them to the least-significant positions).

The masks can be defined as follows:

```
public static final int RED   = (255 << 16);
public static final int GREEN = (255 <<  8);
public static final int BLUE  = 255;
```

Then, the components can be extracted as follows:

```
    rr = (color & RED)    >> 16;
    gg = (color & GREEN) >>  8;
    bb = (color & BLUE);
```

[PART IV]

Patterns Requiring Advanced Knowledge of Arrays and Arrays of Arrays

Part IV contains programming patterns that require a more advanced understanding of arrays and an understanding of arrays of arrays (sometimes called multi-dimensional arrays). Specifically, this part of the book contains the following programming patterns:

> **Subarrays.** A solution to problems in which calculations must be performed on all of the elements of an array between two indexes.
>
> **Neighborhoods.** A solution to problems in which calculations must be performed on all of the elements of an array that are “near” a particular index.

Both of these patterns involve performing calculations on a subset of the elements in an array. They differ in the way the subset is defined.

Patterns Requiring Advanced Knowledge of [illegible] Arrays

[19]

Subarrays

One of Java's most convenient features is the `length` attribute associated with each array. Because of this feature, it isn't necessary to pass both the array and its length to a method (as it is in some other languages). However, it leads to people creating methods with inflexible signatures. The subarray pattern is a way to remedy this shortcoming.

Motivation

Most of the examples of arrays that you have seen probably involve iterating over all of the elements. However, there are many situations in which you only need to iterate over some of the elements in the array. Unfortunately, because you have only/mostly been exposed to examples in which this isn't the case, you may have started to use a pattern that makes this difficult (and, hence, is sometimes called an *anti-pattern*).

Review

Suppose you were asked to write a method that is passed an array of `int` values and returns the total. You would probably use an accumulator (see Chapter 13) as in the following method:

```
public static int total(int[] data) {
    int result;
```

```
        result = 0;

        for (int i = 0; i < data.length; ++i) {
            result += data[i];
        }
        return result;
    }
```

This method takes advantage of the fact that the number of iterations is determinate (or definite) and uses a `for` loop. This method also takes advantage of the fact that the array has a `length` attribute and, so, does not include it in its signature.[1]

The problem with this implementation is that it does not allow you to find the sum of a subset of the elements. For example, if the indexes represent months and the elements represent sales data, then you might want to find the total sales for only the second quarter (i.e., April, May, and June; 0-based months 3, 4, 5).

Thinking About The Problem

Obviously, what you need to do is add formal parameters to the method that describe the subset of interest. You could, for example, pass another array that contained the indexes to consider. Or, you could pass a conformal `boolean[]` array that contains `true` for the elements to use and `false` for the elements to ignore. In practice, however, both of these solutions are more complicated than is necessary because the most common need is to iterate over a contiguous subset of the elements (i.e., loosely speaking, a subset that contains no "gaps", or a subset in which the difference between two sequential is exactly 1).

The Pattern

The easiest way to solve this problem of iterating over a contiguous subset of the elements is to add two formal parameters, the index to start with and the size of the subset.[2]

1. If you have not yet learned about the `length` attribute, you can instead invoke the `Array.getLength()`, passing it the array.
2. You could, instead, have the second parameter contain the

Traditionally, the index to start with is thought of as an offset from 0 and, hence, is named `offset`. The size of the subset is traditionally named `length`.

The example of monthly sales data can be illustrated as in Figure 19.1. As is apparent from this illustration, the bounds on the loop control variable are now going to be `offset` and `offset + length`. As is also apparent from the illustration, you have to be careful to use a strong inequality when comparing the loop control variable to the upper bound (i.e., < rather that <=) to avoid an off-by-one defect. So, the loop control variable will be initialized to `offset` and the iterations will continue as long as the loop control variable is strictly less than `offset + length`.

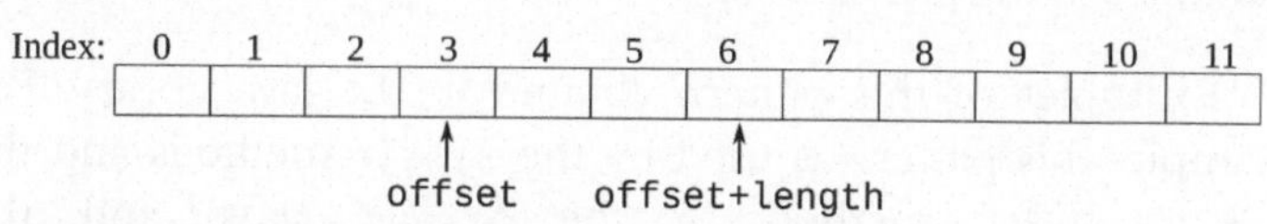

Figure 19.1. The Parameters for the Second Quarter of a Year of Monthly Data

The one drawback of adding these parameters is that they must be included in every invocation of the method. To avoid this, you can add an overloaded version of the method that is only passed the array and invokes the three-parameter version, passing it `0` for `offset` and the array's length attribute for `length`.

Examples

It's trivially easy to create and find examples of this pattern.

The Motivating Example

Returning to the example above, the three-parameter version of the method is as follows:

index to end with. The approach discussed here is more common, in part because it eliminates any confusion about whether the end element is or isn't included.

```
public static double total(double[] data, int offset, int length) {
    double result;

    result = 0;
    for (int i = offset; i < offset + length; ++i) {
        result += data[i];
    }
    return result;
}
```

The one-parameter version then invokes the three-parameter version as follows:

```
public static double total(double[] data) {
    return total(data, 0, data.length);
}
```

Examples in the Java Library

Examples of this pattern abound in the Java library. For example, this pattern is used by the `fill()` methods and the `copyOfRange()` method in the `Arrays` class, and the `arraycopy()` method in the `System` class.

A Less Obvious Example

The same kind of thing can be done with rectangular arrays of arrays (sometimes called multidimensional arrays). In this case, the flexible method is as follows:

```
public static double total(double[][] data,
                           int roffset, int coffset,
                           int rlength, int clength) {
    double result;

    result = 0;
    for (int r = roffset; r < roffset + rlength; ++r) {
        for (int c = coffset; c < coffset + clength; ++c) {
            result += data[r][c];
        }
    }
    return result;
}
```

The one-parameter version then invokes the five-parameter version as follows:

```
public static double total(double[][] data) {
    return total(data, 0, 0, data.length, data[0].length);
}
```

A Warning

It is possible for the invoker to pass an invalid `offset` and/or invalid `length`. Hence, you should validate these parameters and respond to invalid values appropriately.

There are two common responses to invalid values. One is to throw an `IllegalArgumentException`. The other is to use `0` for values of `offset` that are too small, the array's length for values of `offset` that are too large, and the array's length for values of `offset + length` that are too large.

[20]

Neighborhoods

The subarrays pattern, discussed in Chapter 19, considers some problems in which calculations need to be performed on only some of the elements of an array. The solution in that chapter is appropriate only for problems in which the subarray is defined using an offset and a length. This chapter again considers situations in which calculations need to be performed on only some of the elements, but those elements are now conceptualized as a *neighborhood* around a particular element.

Motivation

To *blur* a discretized audio track or visual image, you must calculate the (weighted) average of the elements that are in the neighborhood of a particular element. For an array (which might, for example, contain a sequence of amplitude measurements of an audio track), such neighborhoods have an odd number of elements and are centered on the element of interest. Such a neighborhood is illustrated in Figure 20.1.

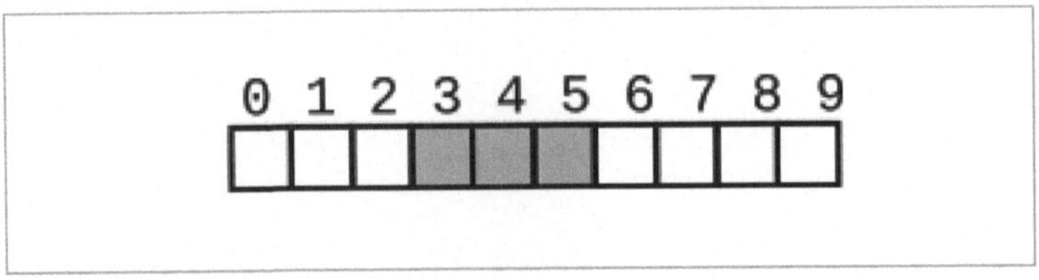

Figure 20.1. A Neighborhood of Size 3 around Element 4

For an array of arrays (which might, for example, contain the color values of the pixels in an image), such neighborhoods are square with an odd number of elements, and are centered around the element of interest. Such a neighborhood is illustrated in Figure 20.2.

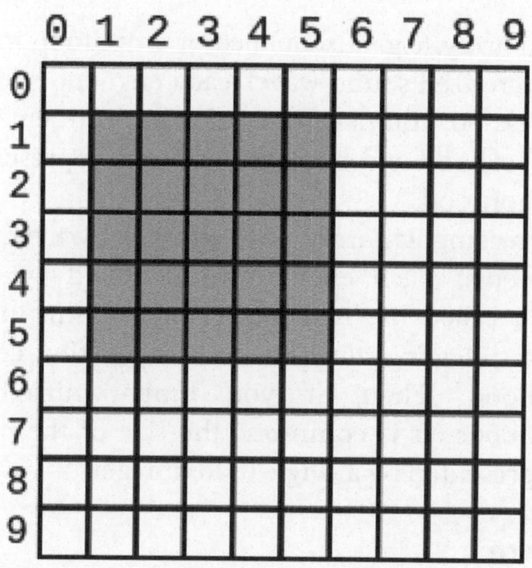

Figure 20.2. A 5×5 Neighborhood around Element $(3, 3)$

Review

If you were to use the subarrays pattern from Chapter 19, you would describe the subset of the elements in Figure 20.1 using an `offset` of `3` and a `length` of `3`. Similarly, you would describe the subset of the elements in Figure 20.2 using a `roffset` (row offset) of `1`, a `coffset` (column offset) of `1`, a `rlength` (row length) of `5`, and a `clength` (column length) of `5`. While there would be nothing technically wrong with this solution, it is not consistent with the conceptual notion of a neighborhood around an element. In other words, it is not consistent with the way domain experts think about the problem.

Thinking About The Problem

When domain experts think about the blurring problem, they think about calculating the weighted average of the elements that are near a center element. Exactly what this means differs with the domain and the dimensionality of the data.

For an array (e.g., a sequence of amplitude measurements from a discretized sound wave), each element is identified by a single index. So, you need one value to represent the center of the neighborhood and one (odd) value to represent the size of the neighborhood.

For a rectangular array of arrays (e.g., a raster/grid of color measurements), each element is identified by two indexes, commonly called the row index and column index. So, you need two integer values to represent the center of the neighborhood. Then, if you limit yourself to square neighborhoods (as is common), the size of the neighborhood can be represented by a single (odd) integer.

The Pattern

As in the subarray pattern of Chapter 19, you need to add formal parameters to the signature of the method you are concerned with. Methods that are passed an array will have two additional parameters (the `index` and the `size`), and methods that are passed an array of arrays will have three additional parameters (the `row` index, `col` index, and `size`).

Also as in the subarrays pattern, you need to calculate the bounds on the loop control variables. While this was quite simple for subarrays, for neighborhoods it's a little more complicated. Returning to Figure 20.1 and Figure 20.2, you can see that you want to have the same number of elements on both sides of the center element. Using integer division, this means that you want to have `size/2` elements on both sides of the center element.

For an array, this means that the lower bound will be given by `index - size/2` and the upper bound will be given by `index + size/2`. For an array of arrays, this means that the lower bound for the rows will be given by `row - size/2`, the upper bound for the rows will be given by `row + size/2`, the lower bound for the columns will be given by `col - size/2`, and the upper bound for the columns will be given by `col + size/2`.

Of course, as always, care must be taken about whether to use a weak inequality or a strong inequality. In this case, a weak inequality is needed to ensure the elements on the boundary are included in the neighborhood. To see why, first consider the array in Figure 20.1. In this example, `index` is `4` and `size` is `3`. So, `size/2` is `1`, meaning that the bounds are `4 - 1` (i.e., `3`) and `4 + 1` (i.e., `5`).

Examples

As always, it's instructive to consider some examples.

Some Obvious Examples

One way to implement the blurring operations discussed in the introduction of this chapter is to use an accumulator (as in Chapter 13) to calculate a neighborhood average. For an array (e.g., a sampled audio clip), this can be implemented as follows:

```
public double naverage(double[] data, int index, int size) {
    double total;
    int    start, stop;

    start = index - size / 2;
    stop  = index + size / 2; // Equivalently: stop = start + size - 1
    total = 0.0;
    for (int i = start; i <= stop; i++) {
        total += data[i];
    }
    return total / (double) size;
}
```

For an array of arrays (e.g., a raster representation of an image), this can be implemented as follows:

```
public double naverage(double[][] data, int row, int col, int size) {
```

```
    double total;
    int    cstart, cstop, rstart, rstop;

    rstart = row - size / 2;
    rstop  = row + size / 2;
    cstart = col - size / 2;
    cstop  = col + size / 2;

    total = 0.0;
    for (int r = rstart; r <= rstop; r++) {
        for (int c = cstart; c <= cstop; c++) {
            total += data[r][c];
        }
    }
    return total / (double) (size * size);
}
```

A Less Obvious Examples

You might also need to use a "plus-sign-shaped neighborhood" in which only the elements in the row or column of the center element are included. You could, use an `if` statement to include only the appropriate elements. Alternatively, you could use two loops, one that iterates over the elements with the same row and one that iterates over the elements that have the same column, as follows:

```
public double paverage(double[][] data, int row, int col, int size) {
    double total;
    int    count, cstart, cstop, rstart, rstop;

    rstart = row - size / 2;
    rstop = row + size / 2;
    cstart = col - size / 2;
    cstop = col + size / 2;

    total = 0.0;
    count = 0;
    for (int r = rstart; r <= rstop; r++) {
        total += data[r][col];
        ++count;
    }
    for (int c = cstart; c <= cstop; c++) {
        total += data[row][c];
        ++count;
    }

    // Eliminate the double counting
    total -= data[row][col];
    --count;

    return total / (double) count;
```

```
}
```

Finally, you could use an array (or array of arrays) of indicators, as discussed in Chapter 6, to control which elements are included. The shape and size of the indicator array (or array of arrays) would correspond to the shape and size of the neighborhood. Indexes to be included in the calculation would have an indicator of `1` and indexes to be excluded would have an indicator of `0`. The indicator would then be multiplied by the calculation. Regardless of the approach, you have to correctly count the elements that are in the total.

Using the Subarray Pattern

Obviously, the neighborhoods pattern and the subarray pattern are closely related, even though they differ conceptually and in the particular parameters that are used. Hence, one can easily combine them. For example, the method for calculating the neighborhood average could use the method for calculating the total of a subarray, rather than duplicate that code, as follows:

```
public double naverage(double[] data, int index, int size) {
    double sum;
    int offset;

    offset = index - size / 2;
    sum = total(data, offset, size);

    return sum / (double) size;
}
```

There is one important subtlety here that you shouldn't ignore. The intervals in the neighborhood pattern are closed whereas the intervals in the subarray pattern are half open (i.e., open on the right).

A Warning

As with the subarray pattern of Chapter 19, the invoker can pass invalid parameters. Hence, you should validate these parameters and respond to invalid values appropriately (either by throwing an exception or using valid default values).

[illegible]

[illegible] the [illegible] and the [illegible]

[illegible]

[illegible]

[PART V]

Patterns Requiring Knowledge of String Objects

Part V contains programming patterns that require an understanding of `String` objects. Specifically, this part of the book contains the following programming patterns:

> **Centering.** Solutions to problems that involve the centering of content (of various kinds) in containers (of various kinds).
>
> **Delimiting Strings.** Solutions to problems that are similar to the problem of inserting commas between the words in a list.
>
> **Dynamic Formatting.** A solution to problems that require the format of a `String` to be determined dynamically (i.e., at run-time rather than at compile-time).
>
> **Pluralization.** A solution to the problem of creating both regular and irregular pluralizations.

The first three patterns in this part of the book all use an accumulator and some other logic to solve their associated problems. The pluralization pattern is really nothing more than a clever use of methods.

[21]

Centering

Many applications need to center content (of some kind) inside a container (of some kind). Though the content and the containers can vary dramatically, the pattern used to do the centering is very consistent.

Motivation

Suppose you have some text that you need to display on the console, centered on the line containing it. Since the console (typically) uses a fixed-width font, the width of every character (measured in pixels) is the same. As a result, both the width of the text and the width of the line can be measured in characters. Your objective, then, is to determine the column of the line that should contain the first character of the text.

Review

The text in this example is going to be represented as a `String` object. So, you can use its `length()` method to determine the number of characters in it. Unfortunately, you have no way of specifying the column of the display to print to when writing to the console.[1] Hence, you have to create or

1. This is not true of all consoles. Some allow you to use control sequences to specify the column (and row) to write

output a `String` that is padded on the left with the appropriate number of spaces, which you can do using an accumulator (see Chapter 13). The only problem that remains, then, is the determination of the appropriate number of spaces.

Thinking About The Problem

Suppose that the line is nine characters wide and 0-based (i.e., the first character is at position 0). Then, you know that the middle character in the line has index `4` (i.e., `9 / 2`, using integer division), since there are four characters to the left of index `4` and four characters to the right of index `4`.

Suppose further that the text is five characters wide and is also 0-based. Then, you know that the middle character of the text has index `2` (i.e., `5 / 2`), since there are two characters to the left of index `2` and two characters to the right of index `2`.

So, in order to center the text in the line, you want character `2` of the text to be at position `4` of the line. This means that character `0` of the text must be at position `2` of the line.

The Pattern

The centering pattern is nothing more than a generalization of this example. First, instead of text, you should think more generally about content. Second, instead of a line, you should think more generally about a container. Both the content and the container have an *extent* that generalizes the notion of the width in the example, and a *reference* that generalizes the notion of a starting character.

The centering problem is to find the reference for the content, given the reference and extent of the container and the extent of the content. Letting C denote the container, c denote the content, and the superscripts R, E and M denote the reference, extent, and midpoint respectively (for each dimension), the centering pattern involves three steps.

to. However, these capabilities are not normally discussed in introductory programming courses. In addition, even with such a console, the centering pattern is needed to find the row or column. Such a console just eliminates the need to pad the `String`.

First, you need to calculate the midpoint of the container (which had a reference of 0 and an extent of 9 in the example). You can do this as follows:

$$C^M = C^R + (C^E/2)$$

Next, you need to calculate the midpoint of the content (which had a width of 5 in the example). You can do this as follows:

$$c^M = (c^E/2)$$

Finally, you need to calculate the reference for the content by subtracting the midpoint of the content from the midpoint of the container. That is:

$$c^R = C^M - c^M$$

In one dimension (i.e., when the references and the extents can be represented by a single number) as in the text example, this algorithm can be implemented as follows:

```
public static double center(double containerReference,
                            double containerExtent,
                            double contentExtent) {
    double containerMidpoint = containerReference + containerExtent / 2.0;
    double contentMidpoint = contentExtent / 2.0;
    double contentReference = containerMidpoint -  contentMidpoint;

    return contentReference;
}
```

Of course, many problems are not one dimensional. For example, images and windows have both a width and a height, and their positions are specified with both a horizontal and a vertical coordinate. Fortunately, the logic is exactly the same for all of the dimensions. Hence, if both the extents and the references are represented as conformal arrays (see Chapter 17), then you can perform the calculations for each dimension independently in the body of a loop as follows:

```
public static double[] center(double[] containerReference,
                              double[] containerExtent,
                              double[] contentExtent) {
    int n = containerReference.length;
    double[] contentReference = new double[n];

    for (int i = 0; i < n; ++i) {
        double containerMidpoint = containerReference[i]
            + containerExtent[i] / 2.0;
```

```
            double contentMidpoint = contentExtent[i] / 2.0;

            contentReference[i] = containerMidpoint - contentMidpoint;
        }
        return contentReference;
    }
```

Examples

Unlike the other patterns in this book, for this pattern it is useful to consider some examples that don't involve the use of any code.

A One-Dimensional Example

An example of centering in one dimension is illustrated in Figure 21.1. The upright numbers in this figure are the inputs, and the italicized numbers in this figure are the calculated values. This example might, again, involve centering text, but the objective now is to center the text within a portion of a line (e.g., a field with a given width). In this example, the content (i.e., the text) has a width of 4, and the field has a width of 17 and starts in column 8.

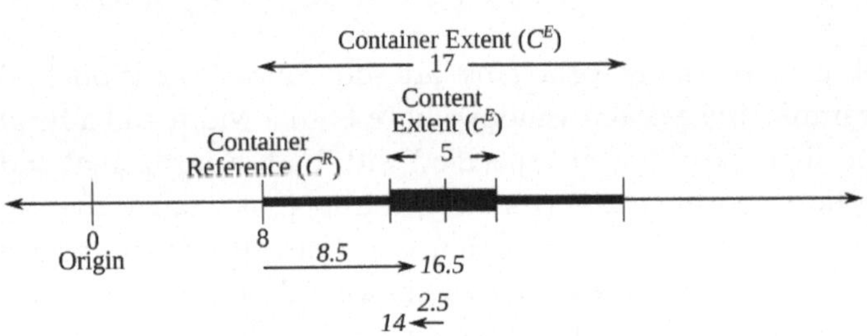

Figure 21.1. Centering in One Dimension

You should begin with the container's reference and the container's extent, and use them to calculate the container's midpoint as follows:

$$\begin{aligned} C^M &= C^R + (C^E/2) \\ &= 8 + (17/2) \\ &= 8 + 8.5 \\ &= 16.5 \end{aligned}$$

In other words, it's necessary to move 8.5 units to the right of the container's reference of 8 to get the container's midpoint of 16.5.

Then, you can calculate the content's reference as follows:

$$\begin{aligned} c^R &= C^M - (c^E/2) \\ &= 16.5 - (5/2) \\ &= 16.5 - 2.5 \\ &= 14 \end{aligned}$$

In other words, it's necessary to move 2.5 units (half of the content's width) to the left of the container's midpoint to get the content's reference.

A Two-Dimensional Example

An example of centering in two dimensions is illustrated in Figure 21.2. Again, the upright numbers are the inputs, while the numbers in italics are calculated. This example might involve centering an image inside of a window in a graphical user interface (GUI). In this context, the content (i.e., the image) has a width of 6 and a height of 8 (i.e., is 6×8), and the container (i.e., the window) has a width of 30 and a height of 12 (i.e., is 30×12).

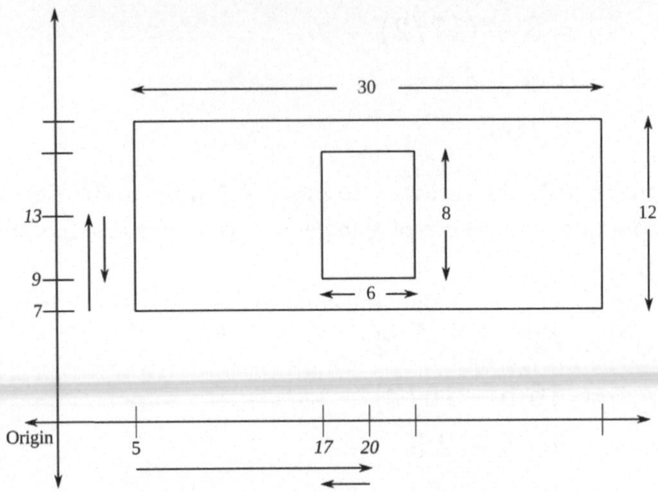

Figure 21.2. Centering in Two Dimensions

Some Warnings

The pattern above can be used in a wide variety of situations, but there are some things that you should be aware of.

Coordinate Systems

All of the figures and examples in this chapter use Euclidean coordinates in which the horizontal coordinates increase from left to right, and the vertical coordinates increase from bottom to top. However, computer graphics tend to use screen coordinates in which the horizontal coordinates increase from left to right but the **vertical coordinates increase from top to bottom**. This means that the sign of the adjustments in the vertical dimension must be negated.

Using Integers

The code above assumes that the references and extents are all `double` values. However, the text example uses `int` values (since the content must be an integer and the column positions are integers). Fortunately, with a little care, the pattern can be used for both `int` values and `double` values.

The first thing to realize is that, if either of the extents is even, then the content can't be perfectly centered. The calculated integer midpoint will either "lean" to the left or the right of the conceptual real-valued center.

The second thing to realize is the impact of integer division and how it differs depending on whether the extent is odd or even. To get started thinking about this issue, just use the pattern exactly as it is implemented above, replacing the `double` values with `int` values, and consider the container and the content individually.

When the **extent of the container** is odd, the calculated midpoint will be at the conceptual center. For example, when the extent is `9` as in the text example above, the midpoint is `9 / 2` or `4`, which leaves 4 characters to the left (i.e., indexes `0`, `1`, `2`, and `3`) and 4 characters to the right (i.e., indexes `5`, `6`, `7`, and `8`). On the other hand, when the extent of the container is even, the calculated midpoint will "lean" right. For example, when the extent is `8`, the midpoint is `8 / 2` or `4`, which leaves 4 characters to the left (i.e., indexes `0`, `1`, `2`, and `3`) but only 3 characters to the right (i.e., indexes `5`, `6`, `7`).

When the **extent of the content** is odd, the calculated midpoint will again be at the conceptual center. For example, when the extent is `5` as in the text example above, the midpoint is `5 / 2` or `2`, which leaves 2 characters to the left (i.e., indexes `0` and `1`) and 2 characters to the right (i.e., indexes `3` and 4). So, the leftward adjustment will be 2 characters. On the other hand, when the extent of the content is even, the calculated midpoint will again "lean" right. For example, when the extent is `4`, the midpoint is `4 / 2` or `2`, which leaves 2 characters to the left (i.e., indexes `0` and `1`) but only 1 characters to the right (i.e., index `3`). So, the leftward adjustment will still be 2 characters.

Putting all of this together, leads to the following conclusions:

1. When the container has an extent of `9`, the reference of the content will be `4 - 2` or `2` whether the content

has an extent of `5` or `4`. Hence, when the content has an extent of `5` it will be exactly centered, and when the content has an extent of `4` it will "lean" to the left by one character.

2. When the container has an extent of `8`, the reference of the content will be `4 - 2` or `2` whether the content has an extent of `5` or `4`. Hence, when the content has an extent of `5` it will "lean" to the right by one character, and when the content has an extent of `4` it will be exactly centered.

In other words, the "lean" will be at most one character (which is as small as it can be).

Of course, if you want the "lean" to be consistently in one direction or the other, then you can adjust the algorithm slightly depending on whether the extents are odd or even. Fortunately, you can easily identify these cases using the arithmetic on the circle pattern discussed in Chapter 4.

Clipping

The examples in this chapter assume that the container is large enough (in all dimensions) to hold the content. When this is not the case, the content may need to be *clipped* to fit in the container. Fortunately, the logic for doing so is straightforward.

[22]

Delimiting Strings

Many programs, whether they have a textual user interface or a graphical user interface, need to combine an array of `String` objects into a single `String` object that has a delimiter between every pair of elements. There are several ways of accomplishing this goal.

Motivation

Suppose you want to generate the `String` object `"Rain,Sleet,Snow"` from a `String[]` containing the elements `"Rain"`, `"Sleet"`, and `"Snow"`. One way to think about the desired result is that there is a comma (the delimiter) between every pair of elements. A second way to think about the desired result is that there is a comma after every item except the last one. A third way to think about the desired result is that there is a comma before every item except the first one. As it turns out, each leads to a different implementation.

Review

Since you are going to iterate over the `String[]` array and consider each element individually, the first conceptualization is a little awkward to deal with. Specifically, you will need to consider both element `i` and `i-1` or `i+1` at each iteration. If you work with index `i-1` you will need to ensure that there are two elements and then initialize the loop control variable to `1`. If you work with index `i+1` you will need to ensure that there are two elements and then terminate the loop at the length of the array minus two. Neither is impossible, but both seem unnecessarily complicated if they can be avoided. Fortunately, both of the other conceptualizations only require you to work with one element at a time using an accumulator (as discussed in Chapter 13) so the first conceptualization won't be considered.

Thinking About The Problem

The other two conceptualizations differ in that one appends the delimiter after concatenating an element to the accumulator, and the other prepends the delimiter before concatenating an element to the accumulator

Appending the Delimiter

The second conceptualization requires you to append the delimiter after every item except the last one. Assuming `item` contains the `String[]` and `delim` contains the delimiter, this can be implemented as follows:

```
// Append the delimiter when needed
result = "";
for (int i = 0; i < item.length; ++i) {
    result += item[i];
    if (i < item.length - 1) {
        result += delim;
    }
}
```

It is also possible to treat an array of length 1 as a special case, initializing the accumulator accordingly, and then start with element 1 as in the following implementation:

```
// Append the delimiter when needed, initializing
// the accumulator based on the length
if (item.length > 1) {
    result = item[0] + delim;
} else if (item.length > 0) {
    result = item[0];
} else {
    result = "";
}
```

```
for (int i = 1; i < item.length - 1; ++i) {
    result += item[i];
    result += delim;
}

if (item.length > 1) {
    result += item[item.length - 1];
}
```

This eliminates the need for an `if` statement within the loop.

Prepending the Delimiter

The third conceptualization requires you to prepend the delimiter before every item except the first one. This can be implemented as follows:

```
// Prepend the delimiter when needed
result = "";
for (int i = 0; i < item.length; ++i) {
    if (i > 0) {
        result += delim;
    }
    result += item[i];
}
```

Again, the `if` statement in the loop can be eliminated by treating element `0` as a special case, as follows:

```
// Prepend the delimiter when needed, initializing
// the accumulator based on the length
if (item.length > 0) {
    result = item[0];
} else {
    result = "";
}

for (int i = 1; i < item.length; ++i) {
    result += delim + item[i];
}
```

The Pattern

At first glance, you might not prefer one solution to the other. However, if you consider a slight variant of the problem, your assessment might change. In particular, suppose you want to be able to use a different delimiter before the last element. Specifically, suppose you want to generate the `String` `"Rain, Sleet and Snow"`. You now need to distinguish the “normal” delimiter (the comma and space) from the "last" delimited (the word "and" surrounded by spaces).

The append approach can be implemented with the `if` statement in the loop as follows:

```
// Append the delimiter when needed
result = "";
for (int i = 0; i < item.length; ++i) {
    result += item[i];
    if (i < item.length - 2) {
        result += delim;
    } else if (i == item.length - 2) {
        result += lastdelim;
    }
}
```

and without the `if` statement in the loop as follows:

```
// Append the delimiter when needed, initializing
// the accumulator based on the length
if (item.length > 2) {
    result = item[0] + delim;
} else if (item.length > 1) {
    result = item[0] + lastdelim;
} else if (item.length > 0) {
    result = item[0];
} else {
    result = "";
}

for (int i = 1; i < item.length - 2; ++i) {
    result += item[i];
    result += delim;
}

if (item.length > 2) {
    result += item[item.length - 2] + lastdelim + item[item.length - 1];
} else if (item.length > 1) {
    result += item[item.length - 1];
}
```

The prepend approach can be implemented with the `if` statement in the loop as follows:

```
// Prepend the delimiter when needed
result = "";
for (int i = 0; i < item.length; ++i) {
    if (i > 0) {
        if (i < item.length - 1) {
            result += delim;
        } else if (i == item.length - 1) {
            result += lastdelim;
        }
    }
```

```
        result += item[i];
    }
```

and without the `if` statement in the loop as follows:

```
    // Prepend the delimiter when needed, initializing
    // the accumulator based on the length
    if (item.length > 0) {
        result = item[0];
    } else {
        result = "";
    }

    for (int i = 1; i < item.length - 1; ++i) {
        result += delim;
        result += item[i];
    }

    if (item.length > 1) {
        result += lastdelim + item[item.length - 1];
    }
```

Whether to have the `if` statement in the loop or not is subject to debate — the implementations that have the `if` statement inside of the loop seem more elegant but are less efficient than those that do not. Choosing between the two implementations that have `if` statements in the loop is easier. The prepend approach requires either nested `if` statements or a single `if` statement with multiple conditions, so the append approach is more elegant.[1]

Choosing elegance over efficiency, this leads to a programming pattern that consists of two methods. One method has three parameters, the `String[]`, the "normal" delimiter, and the "last" delimiter, and uses the append approach. The other method has two parameters, the `String[]` and the delimiter, and simply invokes the three-parameter version. These two methods can be implemented as follows:

```
public static String toDelimitedString(String[] item,
                                       String delim, String lastdelim) {
    String result;

    result = "";
    for (int i = 0; i < item.length; ++i) {
        result += item[i];
```

1. If we wanted to use a different delimiter between the first two elements the better solution might be different. That capability is rarely required, however.

```
        if (i  < item.length - 2) {
            result += delim;
        } else if (i == item.length - 2) {
            result += lastdelim;
        }
    }
    return result;
}

public static String toDelimitedString(String[] item, String delim) {
    return toDelimitedString(item, delim, delim);
}
```

Examples

Delimited strings get used in both the formatting of numerical data and the formatting of textual information. This pattern can easily be used for both.

One common way of formatting data is called *comma separated values* (CSV), which uses a comma as the delimiter between the different fields in a record. Two other common ways of formatting data are tab-delimited and space-delimited. Nothing special needs to be done to handle any of these schemes; simply use the two-parameter version of the method.

When formatting text, there are two common approaches. Both append a comma after every word but the penultimate and ultimate words. Both also append the word "and" after the penultimate word. They differ in whether or not the "and" is preceded by a comma. For example, some style guides use only the word "and" (as in "rain, sleet and snow") while others use both a comma and the word "and" (as in "rain, sleet, and snow"). The last comma is commonly known as the *Oxford comma*. You could change the logic in the solution above to handle the Oxford comma by making the strong inequality a weak inequality and eliminating the `else`. However, it's much better just to change the final delimiter from `" and "` to `", and "`.

[23]

Dynamic Formatting

It is almost impossible to get this far in an introductory programming course without making extensive use of format specifiers (e.g., with the `printf()` method in the `PrintWriter` class or the `format()` method in the `String` class). However, most, if not all, of the format specifiers you have seen and/or used have probably been hard-coded. It turns out that there are many situations in which format specifiers must be created while a program is running.

Motivation

If you want to print all of the elements of a non-negative `int[]` in a field of width 10, it's easy to do so using the format specifier `"%10d"` as follows:

```
for (int i = 0; i < data.length; i++) {
    System.out.printf("%10d\n", data[i]);
}
```

However, now suppose, instead, that you want the field to be as narrow as possible. Since you can't know the value of the elements of the array when you are writing the program, you can't hard-code the format specifier.

Review

Fortunately, you already have some patterns that can help

you solve this problem. First, from the discussion of accumulators in Chapter 13, you know that you can find the largest `int` in an `int[]` named `data` as follows:

```
max = -1;
for (int i = 0; i < data.length; i++) {
    if (data[i] > max) max = data[i];
}
```

Second, from the discussion of digit counting in Chapter 11, you know that you can find the number of digits in an `int` value named `max` as follows:

```
width = (int) (Math.log10(max)) + 1;
```

So, all you need to complete the solution to the dynamic formatting problem is a format specifier.

Thinking About The Problem

Fortunately, the format specifier is a `String` object, and you can construct and manipulate `String` objects while a program is running. For example, returning to the situation in which you want to use a field of width `10`, you could use a `String` variable named `fs` for the format `String` as follows:

```
fs = "%10d\n";

for (int i = 0; i < data.length; i++) {
    System.out.printf(fs, data[i]);
}
```

Now, all you need to do is replace the hard-coded `10` in `fs` with the value contained in a variable.

The Pattern

In particular, what you need to do is use `String` concatenation (or a `StringBuilder` object) to construct the format `String`. Recall that a format specifier has the following syntax:

%[*flags*][*width*][*.precision*]*conversion*

where:

- *flags* is one or more of: - to indicate left-justification, +

to indicate required inclusion of the sign, ,to include grouping separators, etc.

- *width* indicates the width of the field
- *precision* indicates the number of digits to the right of the decimal point for real numbers
- *conversion* is one of `b` for a `boolean`, `c` for a `char`, `d` for an integer, `f` for a real number, `s` for a `String`, etc.

and items in square brackets are optional.

So, assuming all of the variables have been declared, you can construct a format specifier at run-time as follows:

```
fs = "%";
if (flags != null) fs += flags;
if (width > 0)       fs += width;
if (precision > 0) fs += "." + precision;
fs += conversion;
```

Examples

Suppose you want to illustrate the non-repeating nature of the digits of π by printing a table in which the first line contains one digit to the right of the decimal point, the second contains two digits to the right of the decimal point, etc. To accomplish this you need to construct the format specifier inside of a loop, and print `Math.PI` using that format specifier at each iteration. This can be accomplished as follows:

```
for (int digits = 1; digits <= 10; digits++) {
    fs = "%" + (digits + 2) + "." + digits + "f\n";
    System.out.printf(fs, Math.PI);
}
```

Note that this example uses `digits + 2` to account for the leading `3.` in the output.

As another example, suppose you want to create a `String` called `result` from a `String` called `source`, and you want `result` to satisfy the following specifications:

1. It must have `width` characters in total; and
2. The characters in `source` must be centered within `result`.

You know from the discussion of centering in Chapter 21 that there must be `width - source.length()` spaces in `result` with "half" of them to the left of `source` and "half" of them to the right of `source`. This can be accomplished as follows:

```
public static String center(String source, int width) {
    int      field, n, append;
    String   fs, result;

    // Calculate the number of spaces in the resulting String
    n = width - source.length();
    if (n <= 0) return source;

    // Calculate the width of the field for source (it will be
    // right-justified in this field)
    field = (width + source.length()) / 2;

    // Calculate the number of spaces to append to the right
    append = width - field;

    // Build the format specifier
    fs = "%" + field + "s%" + append + "s";

    result = String.format(fs, source, " ");
    return result;
}
```

The `source` will be right justified in a field that is `(width/2 - source.length())/2` characters wide and it will be followed by a single space that will be right justified in a field that is as wide as is necessary to fill the field.

[24]

Pluralization

Programs often need to create output strings that contain different words/phrases depending on the value of an associated integer. There are many different ways to solve this problem, but most of them are awkward, at best.

Motivation

For example, suppose you are writing a program for a local animal shelter that must produce the output "There is 1 poodle available for adoption." when they have one poodle and "There are 3 poodles available for adoption." when they have three poodles. There are two differences between these two sentences: the "is"/ "are" distinction and the "poodle"/ "poodles" distinction, both of which can be thought of as pluralization problems.

Review

You could, of course, treat this as an isolated problem. For example, assuming the variable n contains the number of poodles, you could solve this problem as follows:

```
if (n == 1) {
    result = "There is 1 poodle available for adoption.";
} else {
    result = "There are " + n + " poodles available for adoption.";
```

```
    }
```

However, the amount of duplication in the two `String` literals makes this solution prone to error; typing them both exactly as wanted is difficult and it is easy to make mistakes when copying, pasting, and editing the copy. Hence, you might instead solve this specific problem as follows:

```
result = "There";

if (n == 1) result += " is";
else        result += " are";

result += " " + n + " poodle";

if (n > 1) result += "s";

result += " available for adoption.";
```

Unfortunately, it's easy to get careless (and lazy) in situations like this. Hence, it would be nice to have a more generic solution.

Thinking About The Problem

You'd probably like to be able to construct a `String` in one form (e.g., the singular) and then invoke a method (e.g., `pluralize()`) that converts it to the other form (e.g., the plural). However, this kind of natural language processing (NLP) problem is very difficult to solve, and such a method would be far too computationally burdensome and unreliable for most applications.[1] Fortunately, however, **you** speak English and are very good at converting from one form to another. So, the solution to the problem is to harness your ability to pluralize in a convenient way.

The Pattern

The solution starts with a simple method that returns either the singular or plural form of a word (both of which you provide to the method), based on the value of another parameter:

```
public static String form(int n, String singular, String plural) {
```

1. An artificial/contrived solution of this kind is sometimes called a *Deus ex machina*, which is Latin for "god from the machine".

```
    if (n > 1) return plural;
    else       return singular;
}
```

Then, you simply create a bunch of specific methods that use this method.

Examples

Continuing with the animal shelter example, you first need the following method for the word "is"/ "are":

```
public static String is(int n) {
    return form(n, "is", "are");
}
```

You then need the following method for adding an "s" to regular nouns:

```
public static String regular(int n, String noun) {
    return noun + form(n, "", "s");
}
```

Assuming all of these methods are in a class named `Pluralize`, they can then be used with a regular noun like "poodle" as follows:

```
    result = "There " + Pluralize.is(n) + " "
        + n + " " + Pluralize.regular(n, "poodle")
        + " available for adoption.";
```

and with an irregular noun like "mouse" as follows:

```
    result = "There " + Pluralize.is(n) + " "
        + n + " " + Pluralize.form(n, "mouse", "mice")
        + " available for adoption.";
```

Finally, an irregular noun like "sheep" could either be handled as in the "mouse" example, or as follows:

```
    result = "There " + Pluralize.is(n) + " "
        + n + " sheep available for adoption.";
```

[PART VI]

Patterns Requiring Knowledge of References

Part VI contains programming patterns that require an understanding of objects and references, and parameter passing. Specifically, this part of the book contains the following programming patterns:

> **Chained Mutators.** A solution to the problem of invoking multiple different methods on the same object, one right after another.
>
> **Outbound Parameters.** A solution to the problem of needing to return multiple pieces of information from a single method.
>
> **Missing Values.** A solution to the problem of distinguishing missing values from actual values so that they can be handled differently when performing calculations of various kinds.
>
> **Checklists.** A solution to the problem of checking to see whether a specific set of criteria (identified at run-time) have been satisfied.

The chained mutators pattern involves the return of a reference, while the outbound parameters pattern involves passing references. The missing values pattern takes advantage of the “special” reference `null`. Finally, the checklists pattern is a generalization of the bit flags pattern that allows for the set of criteria to be created dynamically (i.e., at run-time).

[25]

Chained Mutators

Examples abound in which a method is invoked on the value returned by another method without assigning the returned value to an intermediate variable. Opinions differ, among programmers at all levels, about the efficacy of this practice. Nonetheless, it is quite common. Hence, it is important to consider how this behavior can be taken into account when implementing methods that might be chained in this way.

Motivation

Suppose you need to construct an email address from a `String` variable named `user` containing the user's name and a `String` variable named `university` containing the university's name. Suppose, further, that for efficiency reasons you want to use a `StringBuilder` rather than `String` concatenation.

One way to implement this is as follows:

```
StringBuilder sb = new StringBuilder();
sb.append(user);
sb.append("@");
sb.append(university);
sb.append(".edu");
```

In this implementation, each call to `append()` simply modifies the state of the `StringBuilder` as required.

While this works, it's somewhat messier than using `String`

concatenation, because it requires multiple statements. What you might like to do, instead, is take advantage of the efficiency of the `StringBuilder` class without the added messiness. In principal, you could accomplish this using invocation chaining as follows:

```
StringBuilder sb = new StringBuilder();
sb.append(user).append("@").append(university).append(".edu");
```

However, this will only work if the `append()` method is implemented with this kind of functionality in mind.

Review

Now, consider a different, but related, example. Suppose you are working with a `File` object that encapsulates the current working directory, and you want to know how many characters are in its name. This can be accomplished as follows:

```
File   cwd    = new File(".");
String path   = cwd.getCanonicalPath();
int    length = path.length();
```

However, since there's no need for the intermediate variable `path`, many people prefer the following chained implementation:

```
File   cwd    = new File(".");
int    length = cwd.getCanonicalPath().length();
```

This chained implementation works because the `getCanonicalPath()` method in the `File` class returns (and evaluates to) a `String` object, and the `String` class has a `length()` method.

Thinking About The Problem

Though they are similar on the surface, the email example and the path example are quite different. In the path example, the methods do not change the state of their owning objects. That is, the `getCanonicalPath()` method is an accessor not a mutator (i.e., it does not change the state of its `File` object, it returns a `String` object) and the `length()` method is also an accessor not a mutator (i.e., it does not change the state of its

`String` object, it returns an `int`). On the other hand, in the email example, the `append()` method **does** change the state of its `StringBuilder` (i.e., it is a mutator and does not **need to** return anything).

So, while it is easy to see why you can use invocation chaining in the path example, it does not seem like you should be able to do so in the email example. Indeed, in order for you to be able to use invocation chaining in the path example, the `append()` method must return the `StringBuilder` that it is modifying.

The Pattern

This motivating example can be generalized to create a pattern that solves the chained mutator problem. Specifically, if you want to be able to use invocation chaining to change an object, then the mutator methods that are to be chained must return something that a subsequent method in the chain can be invoked on. But, it can't just return anything; it must return an object of the appropriate type (i.e., an object of the same type as the owning object). But, even that isn't enough — it must actually return the owning object itself. That is, the mutator must return the reference to the owning object, `this`.

The `StringBuilder` class uses this idea, for exactly this reason. The methods `append()`, `delete()`, `insert()`, `replace()`, and `reverse()` all return `this` so that their invocations can be chained. So, in the example, `sb.append(user)` returns `this` (i.e., a reference to `sb`), `append("@")` is then invoked on `sb`, and so on.

An Example

Suppose you want to create an encapsulation of a `Robot` that keeps its location in one or more attributes and is able to move in four directions (forward, backward, right and left). You clearly need one or more mutator methods to handle the movements. Suppose further that you decide to have a mutator method for each direction, named `moveBackward()`, `moveForward()`, `moveLeft()`, and `moveRight()`.

If you were not interested in supporting invocation

chaining, then these methods would be `void` (i.e., they would not return anything), and they could be used as in the following example:

```
Robot bender = new Robot();
bender.moveForward();
bender.moveForward();
bender.moveRight();
bender.moveForward();
```

However, if you are interested in invocation chaining, these methods must, instead, return a reference to the owning object, as in the following implementation:

```
public class Robot {
    private int x, y;

    public Robot() {
        x = 0; y = 0;
    }

    public Robot moveBackward() {
        y--;
        return this;
    }

    public Robot moveForward() {
        y++;
        return this;
    }

    public Robot moveLeft() {
        x--;
        return this;
    }

    public Robot moveRight() {
        x++;
        return this;
    }

    public String toString() {
        return String.format("I am at (%d, %d).", x, y);
    }
}
```

You can then use this object as follows:

```
Robot bender = new Robot();
bender.moveForward().moveForward().moveRight().moveForward();
```

Many people think the chained invocation is much more convenient than having to use a separate statement for each movement. If, however, you want to have a separate statement for each movement you can; you just ignore the return value (as in the original example). In other words, providing the ability to chain invocations has no disadvantages, only advantages.

A Warning

It is very important to document chainable mutator methods, and methods that look like chainable mutator methods, carefully. This need is made apparent by the `String` and `StringBuilder` classes.

For example, the `toLowerCase()` and `toUpperCase()` methods in the `String` class could easily be mistaken for mutators. In fact, if you didn't know that `String` objects were immutable, you would almost certainly think this was the case. The clue that they are not mutators is the fact that they return `String` objects. In other words, the fact that they return a `String` object is a clue that they construct a new `String` object from the owning `String` object and return the new object.

As another example, the `Color` class has `brighter()` and `darker()` methods that you might think, from their names, are mutators. Again, however, `Color` objects are immutable, and one clue is that these methods return `Color` objects.

However, it is important not to over-generalize. As you've now seen, many mutator methods in the `StringBuilder` class return `StringBuilder` objects. In this case, it is to support invocation chaining. The only way to know is to read the documentation.

So, it is very important to carefully document methods in immutable classes that might appear to be mutators and mutators in mutable classes that support invocation chaining. It is easy to make inappropriate assumptions about the way an object will behave, based only on method signatures. The only way to prevent the problems that arise from such assumptions is to document the code.

[26]

Outbound Parameters

Though it is not always discussed in introductory programming courses, parameters can be used to pass information to a method (i.e., inbound parameters), to pass information from a method (i.e., outbound parameters), or to do both (i.e., in-out parameters). While some programming languages make this explicit, Java does not.

Motivation

In Java, a method can only return a single value or reference, and this is sometimes inconvenient. Suppose, for example, you want to write a method that is passed a `double[]` and returns both the maximum value and the minimum value. One way to achieve the desired result is to construct and return a `double[]` that contains two elements, the maximum and the minimum. Another way to achieve the desired result is to create a class called `Range` that contains two attributes, the minimum and maximum, and construct and return an instance of it. This chapter considers a third approach — *outbound parameters.*

Review

In order to understand the use of outbound parameters in Java, it is critical to understand *parameter passing*. In particular, it is critical to understand that Java passes all parameters *by value*. This means that the *formal parameter* (sometimes called the *parameter*) is, in fact, a copy of the *actual parameter* (sometimes called the *argument*). This is important because it means that, though a method can change the formal parameter, it can't change the actual parameter.

Thinking About The Problem

At first glance, this might make you think that it is impossible to have outbound parameters in Java. However, when a parameter is a reference type, even though the formal parameter is a copy of the actual parameter, the formal and actual parameters refer to the same object. That is, they are *aliases*. Hence, if the object is mutable, a method can change the attributes of that object.

With this in mind, there are three different situations to consider, corresponding to the need to pass each of the following:

1. A mutable reference type;
2. A value type; or
3. An immutable reference type.

Each situation must be handled slightly differently.

The first situation is the easiest to handle. In this case, the method simply changes the attributes of the outbound formal parameter (which is an alias for the actual parameter).

The second situation is slightly more complicated. In this case, changing the formal parameter has no impact on the actual parameter. What you'd like to do is, somehow "convert" the value type to a reference type. While this isn't possible, you can, instead, create a *wrapper class*, that serves the same purpose. For example, if you want to have an outbound `int` parameter then you write an `IntWrapper` class like the following:

```
public class IntWrapper {
    private int   wrapped;

    public IntWrapper() {
        set(0);
    }
```

```
    public IntWrapper(int i) {
        set(i);
    }

    public int get() {
        return wrapped;
    }

    public void set(int i) {
        wrapped = i;
    }
}
```

The third situation is more like the second than the first. Since the parameter is immutable, even though the formal parameter is an alias, there is no way to change the attributes of the object being referred to. Hence, you must again create a wrapper class. For example, if you want to have an outbound `Color` parameter (which is immutable) then you write a `ColorWrapper` class like the following:

```
import java.awt.Color;

public class ColorWrapper {
    private Color wrapped;

    public ColorWrapper() {
        set(null);
    }

    public ColorWrapper(Color c)
    {
        set(c);
    }

    public Color get() {
        return wrapped;
    }

    public void set(Color c) {
        wrapped = c;
    }
}
```

The Pattern

What all of this means is that to make use of this pattern you must complete several steps.

1. Write a wrapper class if necessary;
2. Declare a method with an appropriate signature;

3. (See below);
4. Perform the necessary operations in the body of the method; and
5. Modify the attributes of the outbound parameter.

To use the pattern in this form, the invoker of the method must then construct an "empty" instance of the outbound parameter and pass it to the method. When the method returns, the values of the outbound parameter will have been set, and the invoker can then make use of it.

The solution can be improved by giving the invoker the flexibility to either use an outbound parameter for the result or to return the result. The invoker can signal its preference by passing either an empty/uninitialized outbound object or `null`. In the latter case, the method will construct an instance of the outbound parameter, modify it, and return it. In the former case, the method will modify the given outbound parameter, **and return it** (for consistency).

This leads to the following additional steps (which you may have noticed are missing above):

3. At the top of the method, check to see if the outbound parameter is `null` and, if it is, construct an instance of the outbound parameter;
6. Return the outbound parameter.

Examples

Some examples will help to clear up any confusion you may have.

Outbound Arrays

Returning to the motivating example, if you want to simultaneously calculate the minimum and maximum elements of a `double[]`, you can use the pattern to create an `extremes()` method like the following:

```
public static double[] extremes(double[] data, double[] range) {
    if (range == null) range = new double[2];

    range[0] = Double.POSITIVE_INFINITY;
    range[1] = Double.NEGATIVE_INFINITY;
```

```
    for (int i = 0; i < data.length; i++) {
        if (data[i] < range[0]) range[0] = data[i];
        if (data[i] > range[1]) range[1] = data[i];
    }

    return range;
}
```

You can then invoke this method in either of two ways.

On the one hand, you can construct the array to hold the outbound parameter as follows:

```
double[] temperatures = {75.3, 81.9, 68.2, 67.9};
double[] lowhigh = new double[2];

extremes(temperatures, lowhigh);
```

The variable that was constructed to contain the outbound parameters can then be used normally. In this case, `lowhigh[0]` will contain the minimum, and `lowhigh[1]` will contain the maximum.

On the other hand, you can pass `null` as the outbound parameter and allow the method to construct and return it, as follows:

```
double[] temperatures = {75.3, 81.9, 68.2, 67.9};
double[] lowhigh;

lowhigh = extremes(temperatures, null);
```

After the return, `lowhigh` can be used exactly as in the previous example. The difference is that the memory for the array was allocated in the method named `extremes()` rather than in the invoker.

Note that it is not necessary to pass `null` explicitly. One can, instead, pass a variable that has been assigned the reference `null`, as in the following example:

```
double[] temperatures = {75.3, 81.9, 68.2, 67.9};
double[] lowhigh = null;

lowhigh = extremes(temperatures, lowhigh);
```

The difference is purely stylistic, though some people prefer the explicit approach for clarity reasons.

Outbound Mutable Objects

Continuing with the same example, instead of using an array for the outbound parameter, you can create a class of mutable objects named `Range` to accomplish the same thing, as follows:

```
public class Range {

    private   double max, min;

    public Range() {
        set(Double.NEGATIVE_INFINITY, Double.POSITIVE_INFINITY);
    }

    public Range(double min, double max) {
        set(min, max);
    }

    public double getMax() {
        return max;
    }

    public double getMin() {
        return min;
    }

    public void set(double min, double max) {
        this.min = min;
        this.max = max;
    }
}
```

The method for finding the minimum and maximum (now named `extrema()` rather than `extremes()` to avoid any confusion) can then be implemented as follows:

```
    public static Range extrema(double[] data, Range range) {
        if (range == null) range = new Range();
        double  max, min;

        min = Double.POSITIVE_INFINITY;
        max = Double.NEGATIVE_INFINITY;

        for (int i = 0; i < data.length; i++) {
            if (data[i] < min) min = data[i];
            if (data[i] > max) max = data[i];
        }
        range.set(min, max);
        return range;
    }
```

It can then be invoked with a second parameter that is explicitly null or a Range variable that has been assigned the value null as in the earlier example.

Should you want to include both versions (i.e., the one that is passed/returns a double[] and the one that is passed/returns a Range) and want to be able to explicitly pass null as the second parameter, then the two methods must have different names. Otherwise, the invocation will be ambiguous (i.e., the compiler will not be able to determine which version you want to invoke because null does not have the type of the second parameter in either version).[1]

Outbound Value Types

Now suppose that you want to write a method that is passed an int[] and calculates the number of positive elements, the number of negative elements, and the number of zeroes. You could return an array containing these values, but this approach is prone to error because you must remember which index corresponds to which value. So, you decide to use outbound parameters.

However, as discussed above, you can't use int values directly; instead you must use a wrapper. This leads to the following implementation:

```
public static void summarize(int[] data,
                             IntWrapper positives,
                             IntWrapper negatives,
                             IntWrapper zeroes) {
    int neg = 0, pos = 0, zer = 0;

    for (int i = 0; i < data.length; i++) {
        if (data[i] < 0) neg++;
        else if (data[i] > 0) pos++;
        else zer++;
    }
    positives.set(pos);
    negatives.set(neg);
    zeroes.set(zer);
}
```

Note that, in this example, the method doesn't return anything. Hence, the invoker must construct the outbound parameters.

1. You could type cast null as either a double[] or a Range to resolve the ambiguity, but that's inconvenient.

Outbound Immutable Objects

Finally, suppose that you are obsessed with your University's color palette (e.g., purple and gold), and that you want to write a method that converts any `Color` to the main color in that palette (e.g., purple). Since `Color` objects are immutable, you must wrap the parameter as discussed above. You can then implement the `purpleOut()` method as follows:

```
public static ColorWrapper purpleOut(ColorWrapper wrapper) {
    if (wrapper == null) wrapper = new ColorWrapper();

    wrapper.set(new Color(69, 0, 132));
    return wrapper;
}
```

It can then be invoked as follows:

```
    ColorWrapper color = new ColorWrapper(Color.RED);

    purpleOut(color);
```

A Warning

You might be wondering why you had to write an `IntWrapper` class when the Java API includes the `Integer`, `Double`, `Boolean`, etc. classes. While those classes are also wrappers, they were designed for a different purpose. Specifically, they were created so that wrapped value types could be added to collections (which hold references). As it turns out, the objects in those classes are immutable and, hence, can not be used for the purposes of this chapter.

[27]

Missing Values

When working with numeric data one often needs to deal with missing values. Failing to take this requirement into account early in the development process can cause enormous problems later on.

Motivation

Suppose you're writing a program that helps households manage their monthly budgets (in dollars and cents). Users of such a program have to enter their various expenditures every week. Unfortunately, people sometimes forget to do so. For example, someone might forget to enter their grocery expenditures for a particular week. When calculating their average expenditure on groceries, this missing value shouldn't be treated as a `0.00`, because that would skew the result. However it must be accounted for somehow.

To deal with problems of this kind you must think about two things. First, you have to think about how to represent missing values. Second, you have to think about how to incorporate them into calculations of various kinds.

Review

If you were given the task of writing such a budget program, you would almost certainly use a `double` to represent expenditures. Then, since expenditures must be non-negative, you would use a sentinel value like `-1.00` to indicate that the expenditure is actually missing.

There are two shortcomings of this approach for general situations. The first, and most important, is that in many situations there is no `double` value that can be used reliably as a sentinel because every possible `double` value is valid.[1] The second is that it is error prone. Specifically, if at some point a programmer forgets to check to see if a value is a sentinel it will be used as if it is valid, resulting in incorrect results (and a defect that is very difficult to localize and correct).

Thinking About The Problem

Ideally, every data type would have an associated sentinel. Unfortunately, this isn't the case. Fortunately, however, all reference types do have an associated sentinel, the reference `null`.

This means that you have a natural way to indicate that something is missing for everything that is represented using a reference type. For example, if you don't have the name of the grocery store where a purchase was made, you can indicate that by assigning `null` to the relevant variable.

The Pattern

This observation leads to a solution to the general problem. Specifically, as in Chapter 26 on outbound parameters, you can use wrapper objects to hold the numeric values. When a particular data point is missing the wrapper object will be `null`, otherwise the wrapper object will hold the value. Since there is no reason for the wrapper objects to be mutable, unlike Chapter 26, you can use the built-in `Double` and/or `Integer` classes.

1. This is one of the reasons the `Double.parseDouble()` method that converts `String` representations of numbers to `double` values throws a `NumberFormatException` when the parameter does not represent a number. There is no sentinel value that it could return to indicate that there was a problem.

Then, before performing any operation on the wrapped data, you just check to see if the wrapper is `null`, extract the value if it isn't, and take the appropriate actions in either case.

This pattern can be summarized as follows. When collecting the data, you must:

1. Declare a wrapper object to be a `Double` or `Integer` as appropriate.

2. If the information isn't missing, use the static `Double.valueOf()` or `Integer.valueOf()` method to construct the wrapper object.[2]

Then, when processing the data, you must:

3. Determine if the wrapper object is `null`.

4a. If it is, take the appropriate actions for a missing value.

4b. If it isn't, use the wrapper object's `doubleValue()` or `intValue()` to retrieve the value and take the appropriate actions for a non-missing value.

Examples

As an example, consider situations in which you need to calculate the mean of an array of data points (using one or more accumulators as in Chapter 13). Each data point is represented as a `Double` object, as is the result of the calculation (i.e., the mean), so that it can be used in subsequent calculations (e.g., in the calculation of the variance). The situations vary in the way missing values are handled.

Using a Default Value

The first kind of situation is one in which a default value is used in place of any missing elements. This would be appropriate, for example, when calculating the mean exam grade in a course in which all of the exams are required and, hence, the `defaultValue` is `0.0`, as in the following:

2. Note that the constructors in the built-in wrapper classes have been *deprecated*, meaning that they shouldn't be used because they may be removed from the language in the future.

```
total = 0.0;
for (int i = 0; i < data.length; i++) {
    if (data[i] == null) {
        total += defaultValue; // Initialized elsewhere
    } else {
        total += data[i].doubleValue();
    }
}
average = total / (double) data.length;
```

All that is needed in this case is to increase the accumulator named `total` by the `defaultValue` when the element is missing or by the actual value when it isn't.

Ignoring Missing Values

The next kind of situation is one in which missing values are ignored (i.e., each missing value is skipped). This approach might be used, for example, to calculate someone's average weekly grocery bill when they might forget to enter the value for a particular week, as in the following:

```
total = 0.0;
n     = 0;
for (int i = 0; i < data.length; i++) {
    if (data[i] != null) {
        total += data[i].doubleValue();
        n++;
    }
}
average = total / (double) n;
```

In this case it is critical to ensure that the number of non-missing values is used when calculating the mean. A second accumulator, `n`, is used for this purpose.

Propagating the Missing Value

The final kind of situation is one in which missing values are *propagated*. In other words, any calculation involving a missing value results in a missing value. This might be appropriate, for example, when calculating the average state population in the United States. If the population for a particular state is missing, it can neither be ignored nor replaced with a default value. So, the average itself must be missing, as in the following:

```
missing = false;
```

```
total = 0.0;
for (int i = 0; i < data.length; i++) {
    if (data[i] == null) {
        missing = true;
        break; // No reason to continue iterating
    } else {
        total += data[i].doubleValue();
    }
}

if (missing) {
    result = null;
} else {
    result = Double.valueOf(total / (double) data.length);
}
```

In this case, after the loop terminates, you need to know if there were any missing values. Again, a second accumulator (named `missing`) is used for this purpose. Note that, as soon as a missing value is encountered, the loop can be terminated.

A Warning

As a convenience, the Java compiler *boxes* and *unboxes* its wrapper objects. This means that, given the following declarations:

```
double  value;
Double  wrapper;
```

a statement like the following:

```
wrapper = value;
```

is actually converted into the following:

```
wrapper = Double.valueOf(value);
```

and then compiled.

Similarly, a statement like the following:

```
value = wrapper;
```

is actually converted into the following:

```
value = wrapper.doubleValue();
```

and then compiled.

It is very easy for beginning programmers to forget that this happens, and make mistakes as a result. It is also very easy to think that the compiler will box/unbox things that it will not. So, for example, you cannot assign a `double[]` to a `Double[]` or vice versa. So, when first starting out, you should not rely on this "convenience".

Looking Ahead

When you learn about collections you will learn about parameterized classes (i.e., type-safe, generic classes). Though they are almost always taught originally in the context of collections, parameterized classes actually have many other uses.

One example is the `Optional` class in the `java.util` package. It is a wrapper class that has methods like `isEmpty()` and `isPresent()` that can be used to determine if a value is missing or supplied. In addition, it has methods like `orElse()` that return the actual contents for non-missing data and a default for missing data.

[28]

Checklists

In many aspects of life, both personal and professional, it is necessary to determine if a set of criteria have been satisfied/accomplished (e.g., goals have been reached, courses have been taken). One common way to do this is to use a checklist.

Motivation

Suppose you're getting ready to go on vacation; you probably have a number of things that you want to remember to pack (e.g., shirts, socks, pants, and skirts). So, you decide to write a program to help you ensure that you don't forget anything. However, unlike the situations considered in Chapter 10 on bit flags, the program will be provided with the checklist dynamically at run-time (i.e., it isn't known when the program is written and compiled).

Review

To increase the flexibility of the program, you decide to represent the criteria that need to be satisfied/accomplished as a `String[]` named `checklist`, and you populate that array before you start working on the tasks. Then, as you accomplish a task, you enter it into another `String[]` named `accomplished`. Each time you accomplish a task you want to be able to determine whether or not you are done (e.g., whether you have completed all of the tasks in the checklist).

Of course, it's easy to compare a single element of `checklist` with a single element of `accomplished` using the `equals()` method in the `String` class. However, in and of itself, that doesn't solve the problem of determining whether or not you are done. Clearly, the `equals()` method must be invoked iteratively.

Thinking About The Problem

You can determine whether any given element of `checklist` has been accomplished by comparing it with each element in `accomplished`. For example, you can determine whether element `index` of `checklist` has been accomplished as follows:

```
boolean done  = false;
for (int a = 0; a < accomplished.length; a++) {
    if (accomplished[a].equals(checklist[index])) {
        done = true;
        break;
    }
}
```

At the end of this loop, `done` will contain `true` if and only if `checklist[index]` has been accomplished.[1]

This loop can be used to determine whether a single criterion has been satisfied/accomplished. To determine if all of the criteria have been satisfied/accomplished this loop needs to

1. Note that the body of the `if` statement contains a `break` statement. While not necessary (i.e., the fragment would be correct without it), there is no reason to continue iterating after it has been determined that `checklist[index]` has been accomplished. Note also that the body of the loop does not contain an `else` clause that assigns `false` to `done`. Since `done` is initialized to `false` outside of the loop, there is no reason to assign a value to `done` at each iteration. Finally, you should be able to convince yourself that, if the `break` statement was omitted and the `else` clause was included, the fragment would not be correct (i.e., when the loop terminates `done` would always contain the value `accomplished[accomplished.length-1].equals(checklist[index])`).

be nested inside of another loop. Unfortunately, there are many ways to do this incorrectly.

For example, the following implementation returns `false` at the first discrepancy between the two arrays, which may just be a result of a difference in how the two are ordered:

```
for all elements in accomplished {
    for all elements in checklist {
        if the accomplished element does not equal the checklist element {
            return false
        }
    }
}
return true
```

As another example, the following implementation returns `true` as soon as it determines that one item on the checklist has been accomplished:

```
for all elements in accomplished {
    assign false to the accumulator named checked

    for all elements in checklist {
        if the accomplished element equals the checklist element {
            assign true to the accumulator named checked
            break
        }
    }
  if checked is true then return true
}
return false
```

In short, there are many incorrect ways to think about the problem. To get the right answer, you must think carefully about the way the loops are nested, the Boolean expression in the `if` statement, the way in which `break` statements are used, and where `return` statements are located.

The Pattern

For this problem, there are two variants of the pattern. In the first variant, you only want the method to return `true` when all of the items on the checklist have been accomplished. You can solve this variant with a single `boolean` accumulator as follows:

```
    private static boolean checkFor(String[] checklist, String[] accomplished) {
        boolean checked;
```

```
        for (int c = 0; c < checklist.length; c++) {
            checked = false;

            for (int a = 0; a < accomplished.length; a++) {
                if (checklist[c].equals(accomplished[a])) {
                    checked = true;
                    break;
                }
            }
            if (!checked) return false; // An item was not accomplished
        }
        return true; // All items were accomplished
    }
```

Note that this algorithm breaks out of the inner loop as soon as it determines that the checklist item of interest has been accomplished. It returns `false` as soon as it determines that any checklist item was not satisfied/accomplished. Hence, if both loops terminate normally then all of the items on the checklist must have been accomplished and the method returns `true`.

In the second variant of the pattern, you want the method to return `true` when more than `needed` elements of the checklist have been accomplished. For this variant, you can use an `int` accumulator named `count` that keeps track of the number of items on the checklist that have been accomplished, as follows:

```
    private static boolean checkFor(String[] checklist, String[] accomplished,
                                    int needed) {
        int       count;
        count = 0;
        for (int c = 0; c < checklist.length; c++) {
            for (int a = 0; a < accomplished.length; a++) {
                if (checklist[c].equals(accomplished[a])) {
                    ++count;

                    if (count >= needed) return true;
                    else                 break;
                }
            }
        }
        return false; // Not enough items were accomplished
    }
```

Again, this algorithm can break out of the inner loop when it determines that the checklist item of interest has been accomplished. In addition, it can return early when `count` reaches `needed`. However, in this case, an early return means the checklist has been satisfied/accomplished. Hence, if both loops terminate normally then the method returns `false`.

Note that both implementations could be improved by checking to ensure that `accomplished.length` is at least as large is necessary to satisfy/accomplish the checklist (i.e., at least as large as `checklist.length` in the first variant and at least as large as `needed` in the second variant). This improvement was omitted for the sake of simplicity.

Examples

It is useful at this point to consider some examples involving both variants above. In all of these examples, `checklist` contains the elements `"Shirts"`, `"Socks"`, `"Pants"`, and `"Skirts"`.

The Inflexible Variant

First, suppose that `accomplished` contains the elements `"Shirts"`, `"Socks"`, `"Pants"`, `"Dresses"`, and `"Shoes"`. In outer iteration 0, the method checks to see if `"Shirts"` has been accomplished. In inner iteration 0, the method determines that it has been and breaks out of the inner loop. In outer iteration 1, the method checks to see if `"Socks"` has been accomplished. In inner iteration 0, the method determines that it hasn't been, but in inner iteration 1 it determines that it has been and breaks out of the inner loop. The iterations then continue as follows:

c	checklist[c]	a	accomplished[a]
0	Shirts	0	Shirts
1	Socks	0	Shirts
		1	Socks
2	Pants	0	Shirts
		1	Socks
		2	Pants
3	Skirts	0	Shirts
		1	Socks
		2	Pants
		3	Dresses
		4	Shoes

Since `checklist[3]` is not an element of `accomplished`, the local variable `checked` is never assigned the value `true`, and the method returns `false`.

Now, suppose that `accomplished` contains the elements `"Socks"`, `"Shirts"`, `"Skirts"`, and `"Pants"`. In outer iteration 0, the method checks to see if `"Shirts"` has been accomplished. In inner iteration 0, the method determines that it hasn't been, but in inner iteration 1 it determines that it has and breaks out of the inner loop. In outer iteration 1, the method checks to see if `"Socks"` has been accomplished. In inner iteration 0, the method sees that it has been and breaks out of the inner loop. The iterations then continue as follows:

c	checklist[c]	a	accomplished[a]
0	Shirts	0	Socks
		1	Shirts
1	Socks	0	Socks
2	Pants	0	Socks
		1	Shirts
		2	Pkirts
		3	Pants
3	Skirts	0	Socks
		1	Shirts
		2	Skirts

In this case, `checked` is assigned the value `true` in every outer iteration, and the method returns `true`.

The Flexible Variant

Now consider the first example above but with the second variant of the method, when `2` is passed into the formal parameter named `needed` (because, apparently, this person is fully-dressed when wearing any two items in the checklist). In outer iteration 0, the method checks to see if `"Shirts"` has been accomplished. In inner iteration 0, the method determines that it has been, increases `count` to `1`, and breaks out of the inner loop. In outer iteration 1, the method checks to see if `"Socks"` has been accomplished. In inner iteration 0, the method determines that it hasn't been, but in inner iteration 1 it determines that it has been, increases `count` to `2`, determines that `count` is greater than or equal to `needed`, and returns `true`.

Now, consider an example in which `accomplished` contains the elements `"Dresses"` and `"Shirts"`. These iterations will proceed as follows:

c	checklist[c]	a	accomplished[a]
0	Shirts	0	Dresses
		1	Shirts
1	Socks	0	Dresses
		1	Shirts
2	Pants	0	Dresses
		1	Shirts
3	Skirts	0	Dresses
		1	Shirts

In inner iteration 1 of outer iteration 0 the method determines that `"Shirts"` have been packed, and increases `count` to 1. However, none of the inner iterations for outer iteration 1 correspond to `"Socks"`, none of the inner iterations for outer iteration 2 correspond to `"Pants"`, and none of the inner iterations for outer iteration 3 correspond to `"Skirts"`. So, count is never increased to `2`, and the method returns `false`.

Looking Ahead

Though some thought was given to the efficiency of the algorithms above, many issues were ignored, and none were considered formally. If you take a course on data structures and algorithms, you will consider these kinds of issues in detail. For example, it is interesting to ask whether it is better to sort `checklist` and/or `accomplished`, either partially or completely. It is also interesting to ask whether it is possible to create a more efficient algorithm when the checklist consists of sequential integers.

[illegible]

[illegible]

[illegible]

INDEX

9 789390 013951

Printed at Repro India Ltd.